A Pragmatic Analysis of Norwegian Modal Particles

Summer Institute of Linguistics and
The University of Texas at Arlington
Publications in Linguistics

Publication 113

Editors

Donald A. Burquest
University of Texas
at Arlington

William R. Merrifield
Summer Institute of
Linguistics

Assistant Editors

Rhonda L. Hartell

Marilyn A. Mayers

Consulting Editors

Doris A. Bartholomew
Pamela M. Bendor-Samuel
Desmond C. Derbyshire
Robert A. Dooley
Jerold A. Edmondson

Austin Hale
Robert E. Longacre
Eugene E. Loos
Kenneth L. Pike
Viola G. Waterhouse

A Pragmatic Analysis of Norwegian Modal Particles

Erik E. Andvik

A Publication of
The Summer Institute of Linguistics
and
The University of Texas at Arlington
1992

© 1992 by the Summer Institute of Linguistics, Inc.
Library of Congress Catalog No: 92–60901
ISBN: 0–88312–188–3
ISSN: 1040–0850

All Rights Reserved

No part of this publication may be reproduced, stored in a retrieval system, or transmitted in any form or by any means—electronic, mechanical, photocopy, recording, or otherwise—without the express permission of the Summer Institute of Linguistics, with the exception of brief excerpts in journal articles or reviews.

Cover design by Hazel Shorey

Copies of this and other publications of the Summer Institute of Linguistics may be obtained from

International Academic Bookstore
7500 W. Camp Wisdom Road
Dallas, TX 75236

To Elin and Maria

Contents

Acknowledgments ix
1. The Norwegian Modal Particles 1
   1.1 Description in traditional grammars 2
   1.2 Stressed near-homophones 4
   1.3 Delimiting modal particles in Norwegian 7
      1.3.1 Modal particles vs. sentence adverbials 7
      1.3.2 Problematic borderline cases 14
      1.3.3 Sentence-final usages 16
   1.4 Regional variety considerations 19
   1.5 Historical features 21
2. Review of the Literature 23
   2.1 German particle research 23
      2.1.1 Particles in traditional grammar 24
      2.1.2 Modern approaches 26
   2.2 Other modal particle research 33
3. Theoretical Framework 35
   3.1 Grice's theory of implicature 36
      3.1.1 Conversational implicatures 36
      3.1.2 Particles as hedges on conversational maxims 38
   3.2 Speech act theory 39
      3.2.1 Truth conditions 39
      3.2.2 Particles as hedges on illocutionary force 40
   3.3 Conversation analysis 41
   3.4 Data corpus 42

4. A Functional Analysis of *jo* and *nå* 45
   4.1 *Jo* 45
      4.1.1 Reduction from *jo* as response particle 45
      4.1.2 The basic meaning of MP *jo* 49
      4.1.3 Supportive *jo* 61
      4.1.4 Oppositional *jo* 66
      4.1.5 Concessive *jo* 69
      4.1.6 Contra-expectational *jo* 72
      4.1.7 Reanalysis: *jo* as oppositional 75
      4.1.8 Conclusion 85
      4.1.9 *Jo* in monologue text 86
   4.2 *Nå* 87
      4.2.1 Reduction from *nå* as adverb 87
      4.2.2 The basic meaning of MP *nå* 91
      4.2.3 Emotional and attitudinal effects 101
      4.2.4 Summary 112

5. Discussion and Conclusions 113
   5.1 Modal particles versus sentence adverbials 113
      5.1.1 Iconicity 114
      5.1.2 The three functional realms 115
      5.1.3 Semantic reduction 116
      5.1.4 Relevance, generality, and phonological reduction . . . 117
   5.2 *Jo* and *nå:* A comparative analysis 119
   5.3 Interaction as manipulation 121
      5.3.1 The speech act ASSERTION revised 123
      5.3.2 *Jo* and *nå* as hedges on felicity conditions 124
   5.4 Implications 128

References 131

Acknowledgments

I wish to extend my deepest appreciation to Dr. Robert E. Longacre for being an example and an inspiration to me throughout my academic program, and especially for his enthusiastic interest in my thesis topic which is the basis for this volume. My thanks to him, to Dr. Jerold A. Edmondson, and Dr. Shin Ja Hwang for their insightful suggestions and encouraging comments.

Finally, my greatest debt of gratitude is to Elin Andvik, my wife and friend, and favorite language informant, who, from the beginning of our relationship, has been patient enough to allow me to interrupt even the most intense conversation with a question about the Norwegian language. I can honestly say, that if it weren't for her, this volume would never have been written.

1
The Norwegian Modal Particles

The focus of this paper is a small class of uninflectable lexical items which occur postverbally, cannot take stress, and have no lexical-semantic reference. They function as an indication of the speaker's attitude toward the proposition or the pragmatic context. Each of these items typically has one or more "near-homophones" (following Arndt 1960) with nonmodal meaning, which may take stress, and which occur with fewer positional restrictions.

There are no literal translations of the particles in English. However, equivalent meanings may usually be expressed by intonation or stress patterns, or by pragmatic devices such as tags. The Norwegian modal particles (MPs) are found in spoken conversation or in written text which represents spoken conversation, such as novels or plays. They are also found in nonformal written text such as personal letters and stories.

The primary goal of this study is to investigate the function of two of the more elusive modal particles, *jo* and *nå*. The claim is made that these constitute an attempt by the speaker to make recourse to an assumed or implied consensus, or commonality, between speaker and addressee. In order to illuminate the function of these, however, some understanding is required of the unique properties of the class of modal particles as a whole. Chapter one therefore presents the entire class, attempting to define and delineate them by means of various criteria, and to differentiate them from other similar expressions of modality. Some of the extensive research done on the historically related German modal particles is surveyed in chapter two, with special emphasis on those works which have made the greatest contribution to the present analysis. Chapter three briefly reviews some central approaches to a pragmatic analysis of the type attempted here, specifically Grice's Theory of Implicature, Austin and

Searle's Speech Act Theory, and the more recent developments in conversation analysis. The actual analysis of the particles *jo* and *nå* is presented in chapter four, beginning with a discussion of their relationship to corresponding stressed near-homophones, and their derivation by semantic and phonological reduction from these near-homophones. This reduction process is taken up again in chapter five, and offered as an explanation for the unique characteristics of the entire class of modal particles. Also in chapter five, the conclusions drawn with regard to *jo* and *nå*, along with a comparative analysis of the two, are summarized, and suggestions are offered for a revision of Searle's felicity conditions on assertions which would allow the consensus particles to be viewed as hedges or modifications on such conditions.

1.1 Description in traditional grammars

Traditional Norwegian grammars for English speakers describe a class of adverbs which in certain contexts take on special meanings or usages which are difficult to translate. These are typically called MODAL ADVERBS. Grammars vary as to which items are to be included in this class.

According to Haugen and Chapman, the modal adverbial usages occur when the item is found unstressed in a sentence, usually at the end of the sentence or immediately following the verb (or an associated pronoun.) In these contexts the modal adverbs take on "special meanings which have no exact equivalents in English," expressing "the speaker's conviction concerning the truth of his statement, and also his emotional attitude toward it or toward the listener" (Haugen and Chapman 1982:305).

Haugen and Chapman include the adverbs *da, jo, nok, nå,* and *vel* in this category whose functions they define as follows:

> *Da* intensifies the statement, suggesting sometimes that the speaker is sympathetic, sometimes that he is impatient. It must usually be omitted in translating into English, though often it can be translated 'certainly, surely', or in questions... 'anyway'.
>
> *Jo* means: the speaker knows that you already know what he is saying—it's a matter of course. It may be translated 'you know' or 'of course'.
>
> *Vel* means that the speaker is quite uncertain and is really asking you whether you agree; in English we repeat part of the question or say 'I suppose'.

Nok means that the speaker isn't quite sure, but believes what he's saying to be true; in English we say 'I guess' or 'all right'.

Nå when used as a modal adverb expresses that the speaker is quite positive about what he is saying. It is used frequently when contradicting, or objecting to, another statement; it can often be translated 'after all'. (Haugen and Chapman 1982:305)

An example sentence from Haugen and Chapman (1982:307) gives the rough English translations for the particles as follows:

(1)   *da*
                 jo
Det   må   nok være massevis av fisk i disse vannene.
                 vel
                 nå
There must x   be   lots   of fish in these lakes.

da: 'Surely there must be lots of fish in these lakes!'
jo: 'Of course there must be lots of fish in these lakes.'
nok: 'There must be lots of fish in these lakes, I suppose.'
vel: 'There must be lots of fish in these lakes, don't you think?'
nå: 'After all, there must be lots of fish in these lakes.'

Stokker and Haddal (1981:465–66) refer to a class of modal adverbs which "when unstressed and immediately following the verb... have the function of changing the mood of the sentence." They include the above with the addition of *visst*, offering the following glosses, or "guidelines," as they put it, for translation.

(2)   *nok*   'all right, probably, to be sure'
       vel   'I suppose, no doubt, of course' (more emphatic than *nok*)
       da   used for emphasis, 'certainly'
       jo   'you know'
       nå   'after all, really'
       visst   'surely, I believe'

Klouman (1984:139) includes yet a larger class of items under his description of the "use of adverbs as modifiers or intensifiers" listed in (3).

(3) vel 'I suppose, probably' (often in questions with uninverted word order)
    jo 'after all, you know'
    da 'then' (but often without any real meaning)
    forresten 'by the way, incidentally, come to think of it'
    nok 'without a doubt, surely'
    liksom 'in a way, kind of, somehow'
    så 'so, such a, such'; in exclamations 'how'

1.2 Stressed near-homophones

Each of the modal particles has a stressed near-homophone with greater distributional freedom, but with a different meaning than its modal particle counterpart. These particles belong to a variety of lexical classes, including adverbials, adjectives, and other types of particles:

Jo when stressed is a response particle 'yes' which functions as the positive answer to a negatively phrased question (cf. German *doch*, French *si*).

(4) *Kommer du ikke?*
    come you not
    Aren't you coming?

    Jo.
    on^the^contrary
    Yes (on the contrary).

Da when stressed is a temporal or logical adverb 'then', 'in that case' or 'thus', as in:

(5) *Da var ikke jeg engang født.*
    then was not I even born
    I wasn't even born then.

    Da prøver vi noe annet.
    then try we something else
    Then (in that case) we'll try something else.

    Vi ser da at svaret er femten.
    we see thus that answer is fifteen
    Thus we see that the answer is fifteen.

Vel when stressed is the adverb or phatic particle 'well'.

(6) *Lev vel!*
  live well
  Live well! (i.e., 'Take care!')

  Han kjørte vel forbi grensen.
  he   drove well beyond border
  He drove well beyond the border.

  Vel... jeg kan prøve.
  well... I   can try
  Well... I can try.

Nok when stressed is the adjective 'enough'.

(7) *Gutten har nok   penger til å kjøpe seg skinnjakke.*
  boy   has enough money to INF buy REFL leather^jacket
  The boy has enough money to buy a leather jacket.

Nå when stressed is the temporal adverb 'now'.

(8) *Jeg er nå en gift   mann.*
  I   am now a married man
  I am now a married man.

  Nå kan du begynne å lasse bilen.
  now can you begin   INF load car
  Now you can start loading the car.

Visst when stressed is a speaker's comment adverb 'certainly'.

(9) *Visst skal våren komme.*
  surely shall spring come
  Surely the spring will come.

Although the stressed near-homophones *da*, *nå*, *nok*, and *vel* may occur in the postverbal position, they are always distinguishable from the modal particles by their nonmodal meaning. In the following examples, the first sentence of each pair contains the stressed near-homophone, the second has the unstressed modal particle.

(10) logical adverb:
Vi har da flere muligheter.
we have thus several possibilities
Thus we have several possibilities.

modal particle:
Vi har da flere muligheter!
we have MP several possibilities
Oh come on, we have more possibilities!

(11) temporal adverb:
Jeg er nå en gift mann.
I am now a married man
I am now a married man.

modal particle:
Jeg er nå en gift mann.
I am MP a married man
After all, I AM a married man.

(12) adjective:
Olsen har nok penger til hus.
Olsen has enough money to house
Olsen has enough money for a house.

modal particle:
Olsen har nok penger til hus.
Olsen has MP money to house
I'm sure Olsen has money for a house.

(13) degree adverb:
Toget går vel forbi Trondheim.
train goes well beyond Trondheim
The train goes well beyond Trondheim.

modal particle:
Toget går vel forbi Trondheim.
train goes MP beyond Trondheim
The train goes past Trondheim, doesn't it?

1.3 Delimiting modal particles in Norwegian

1.3.1 Modal particles vs. sentence adverbials

Givón (1984) defines four types of adverbs. The first three are as follows:

> Manner adverbs: modify the meaning of the verb itself. These have the verb alone under their "semantic scope."

Time adverbs: "characterize the entire event/state, and thus bring the entire sentence under their scope."

Place adverbs: "take under their scope the entire sentence (rather than pertain only to the verb or verb phrase)."

Givón's fourth type of adverb has the widest scope. This type is characterized by the "speaker's comment adverbs," so called because they involve "comments that speakers may make about various aspects of the speech situation." Speaker's comment adverbs are subdivided into three types (Givón 1984:77–79).

1. Comments on desirability or rightness. These "impart the speaker's judgment about either the desirability (from his/her point of view) of the event/state/action or its rightness/wrongness." English examples would be words like unfortunately, luckily, tragically.
2. Comments on the character or motives of the agent. These "impart a variety of judgments the speaker wishes to make about the behavior, character, motives, or habits of the subject/agent participating in an event." English examples here would be excitedly, thoughtfully, deviously, admirably.
3. Epistemic comments. These "impart the speaker's evaluation as to the truth, falsity, possibility or probability of a state or event." Some English examples are probably, surely, maybe, possibly.

According to Givón, the syntactic position of adverbs is often predictable from its semantic scope.

Their syntactic position within sentences varies enormously according to their semantic type, and certain types of adverbs retain considerable word-order flexibility.

To some extent one could predict the degree of word-order flexibility—and in some cases even the syntactic position of adverbs—from their semantic scope... The semantic scope of manner adverbs is the narrowest, essentially taking in only the verb itself. In most languages... these adverbs appear as members of the verb phrase, commonly closest to the verb, and are often incorporated into the verbal word... On the other hand, adverbs with wider—sentential—scope, such as those of time or speaker's comment, tend to have a greater distributional freedom, appearing before, after or in some positions inside the sentence. (Givón 1984:81–82)

Norwegian "speaker's comment" adverbs show the kind of word-order flexibility described above, occurring sentence initially, postverbally, or sentence finally.

(14) *Sannsynligvis kommer pakken idag.*
probably   comes   package today.

Pakken   kommer   sannsynligvis idag.
package comes   probably   today.

Pakken   kommer   idag   sannsynligvis.
package comes   today   probably.

The package will probably come today.

Adverbs of the kind illustrated above have the widest scope in that they convey comments that the speaker is making about some aspect of the speech situation, in this case an "epistemic comment," i.e., "the speaker's evaluation as to the truth, falsity, possibility or probability of a state or event" (Givón 1984:79).

The Norwegian modal particles would appear at first glance to fall under the category of speaker's comment adverbs. They appear to convey a speaker's comment in much the same way as the speaker's comment adverbs. Indeed, as mentioned above, the modal particles are often called modal adverbs in traditional Norwegian grammars (Haugen and Chapman 1982:302, Stokker and Haddal 1981:465). Some of the modal particles, in fact, seem to convey identical meaning to a corresponding modal adverb. The modal particle *nok*, for example, appears to make the same epistemic comment as the adverb *sannsynligvis* 'probably'.

(15) *Pakken   kommer   nok idag.*
package comes   MP today
I suppose the package is coming today.

Likewise the modal particle *visst*, at first glance, is equivalent to the adverb *tilsynelatende* 'apparently'.

(16) *Pakken   kommer   visst idag.*
package comes   MP   today
I guess the package is coming today.

Nevertheless, certain syntactical, morphological, and semantic-pragmatic criteria may be offered to delimit modal particles from modal adverbs. Several of the criteria below are adopted from those set forth by Bublitz (1978) for distinguishing similar German modal particles from modal adverbs, which he calls "modal words."

Syntactic criteria. Modal adverbs may occur at the beginning of sentences, while modal particles may not.

(17) *Sannsynligvis kommer posten sent idag.*
probably comes mail late today
The mail is probably coming late today.

*Nok kommer posten sent idag.
MP comes mail late today
I suppose the mail is coming late today.

Modal adverbs may stand alone as one-word utterances, usually as answers to decision questions of the type, 'Is he there yet? Probably'.

(18) *Er han kommet fram ennå?*
is he come forward yet
Has he arrived yet?

Sikkert.
surely
He must have.

The same question could not be answered by means of a modal particle alone, for example, **nok*, to indicate 'I suppose'. The speaker must couch the attitude-indicating particle within at least a minimal sentence.

(19) *Han har nok det.*
he has MP that
I suppose he has.

Modal adverbs may be focused, while modal particles may not. Consider examples (20)–(21) with utterances and possible responses using modal adverbs.

(20) *Brann tapte sannsynligvis igår.*
Brann lost probably yesterday
Brann probably lost yesterday.

*Ikke bare sannsynligvis; de **har** tapt.*
not just probably they have lost
Not just PROBABLY; they HAVE lost.

(21) *Heldigvis brennte skolen ned.*
fortunately burned school down
Fortunately the school burned down.

*Hvorfor **heldigvis**? Det var synd!*
why fortunately it was too^bad
Why FORTUNATELY? It was too bad!

Now consider examples (22)–(23) with modal particles which may not be focused without losing their modal meaning. In these sets, the response as given cannot occur.

(22) *Brann har nok tapt.*
Brann has MP lost
I suppose Brann has lost.

Ikke bare **nok, de **har** tapt.*
not just MP they have lost
Not just I SUPPOSE, they HAVE lost.

(23) *Skolen brennte visst ned igår.*
school burned MP down yesterday
I guess the school burned down yesterday.

Ikke bare **visst, den **har** virkelig brennt ned.*
not just MP it has really burned down
Not just I GUESS, it really HAS burned down.

Note that these two unacceptable responses may be connected with the inability of modal particles to take stress.

Modal adverbs often have a corresponding derivationally related adjective or verb which conveys the same idea in the form of an adposed clause, as shown in (24) for the modal adverbs *sannsynligvis* 'probably' and *forhåpentligvis* 'hopefully'. This is not true of modal particles—see (25).

(24) *Det er sannsynlig at han kommer.*
　　　it is probable   that he comes
　　　It is probable that he will come.

　　　Jeg håper at   han liker meg.
　　　I   hope that he likes me
　　　I hope that he likes me.

(25) **Det er nok at   han kommer.*
　　　it is MP that he comes
　　　It is supposed that he is coming.

Modal particles may occur in postposed parenthetical clauses, but not in comparative clauses of the type 'as funny AS WAS EXPECTED'. Contrast the following examples:

(26) *Filmen var morsom, som jo var forventet.*
　　　film   was funny,   as MP was expected
　　　The film was funny, as of course was expected.

　　　**Filmen var like morsom som jo var forventet.*
　　　film   was as   funny as   MP was expected
　　　The film was as funny as, of course, was expected.

(27) *Hun var betalt mye, som hun nok forventet.*
　　　she was paid   much as   she MP expected
　　　She was paid much, as I suppose she expected.

　　　**Hun var betalt så mye som hun nok forventet.*
　　　she was paid   as much as she MP expected
　　　She was paid as much as I suppose she expected.

Modal adverbs do not show the same restriction.

(28) *Hun var betalt mye, som hun sannsynligvis forventet.*
　　　she was paid   much as   she probably   expected
　　　She was paid much, as she probably expected.

　　　Hun var betalt så mye som hun sannsynligvis forventet.
　　　she was paid   as much as she probably   expected
　　　She was paid as much as she probably expected.

Morphological criteria. Modal particles are morphologically unchanging, while some modal adverbs can inflect, either morphologically (Bublitz "grammatically") such as *sikrer* 'surer'; or syntactically as *helt sikkert* 'completely sure', *ganske sannsynlig* 'quite probably', but not **ganske nok*.

Modal particles may not take stress without losing their modal meaning. If stress is applied, the item is no longer a modal particle, but a near-homophone of another lexical class, as illustrated above.

Semantic and pragmatic criteria. As Bublitz showed for German, modal particles have no effect on the truth condition of a sentence. This is not the case for those modal adverbs which function as epistemic modifiers. The modal adverb *kanskje* 'perhaps', for example, changes the truth conditions of the proposition.

(29) *Vi vinner lotto denne gang.*
 we win lottery this time
 We'll win the lottery this time.

 Vi vinner kanskje lotto denne gang.
 we win perhaps lottery this time
 Perhaps we'll win the lottery this time.

The above propositions have quite different truth conditions. In contrast, the presence of the modal particle makes no difference in the truth condition of the proposition, because, as will be seen, it functions on a level higher than the proposition itself (cf. Corum 1975:92 for essentially the same claim with reference to Basque particles). The modal particles *nok* and *vel*, although they may seem at first glance to qualify the epistemic content of the proposition, do not in fact change the truth conditions of the proposition, but rather, convey the speaker's personal assessment, i.e., doubt, certainty, etc., regarding the particular utterance in context. Drawing on Krivonosov's idea of SUBJECTIVE modality as CONNOTATIVE meaning (cf. §5.1), we might say that, by means of a modal particle like *nok* or *vel*, the speaker may DENOTE an unqualified assertion, but at the same time CONNOTE that he is not quite sure. This is brought out more fully by the discussion in §5.1, where the claim is made that modal particles carry only a discourse-pragmatic function, having no function on the lexical-semantic nor the propositional level.

When a modal particle occurs in the same sentence as a modal adverb, the modal particle occurs closest to the verb. It is the modal particle which modifies the modal adverb, and never the other way around.

(30) *Han er nok sannsynligvis reist på ferie.*
 he is MP probably   away on vacation
He's probably away on vacation, I suppose.

In sentences where a predicate adjective or locational phrase stands in place of a sentence, the subject and verb having been elipted, modal adverbs such as *sannsynligvis* 'probably' and *tilsynelatende* 'apparently' appear, as in (31a) and (32a), but modal particles do not, as in (31b) and (32b).

(31) a. *Han er trett— sannsynligvis veldig trett.*
  he is tired   probably   very tired
  He is tired—probably very tired.

 b. **Han er trett, nok veldig trett.*
  he is tired MP very tired
  He is tired, I suppose very tired.

(32) a. *Gutten sparket ballen opp på taket. Ja, tilsynelatende*
  boy kicked ball up on roof yes apparently

  helt   opp på taket.
  completely up on roof
  The boy kicked the ball up on the roof. Yes, apparently all the way up on the roof.

 b. **Ja, visst helt   opp på taket.*
  yes MP completely up on roof
  Yes, I guess all the way up on the roof.

1.3.2 Problematic borderline cases

By means of the above criteria, we can identify the postverbal, unstressed occurrences of the following as modal particles: *jo, nå, da, vel, nok,* and *visst. Så* we might eliminate on the grounds that, even unstressed postverbally, it is a degree adverb which modifies the predicate adverb or adjective, and not the clause as a whole.

(33) *Han er så skjønn at   jeg har lyst   å   ta   ham hjem!*
     he   is so cute   that I   have desire INF take him home!
     He is so cute that I'd like to take him home!

   Det går så bra.
   it goes so well
   It will be just fine.

Sikkert 'surely', *liksom* 'sort of', and *forresten* 'by the way' require closer examination. Each may occur unstressed postverbally. Each carries modal meaning. *Sikkert* and *liksom* indicate the speaker's attitude towards the proposition, while *forresten* signals the way in which the speaker intends the proposition to fit into the discourse context. However, in contrast to the modal particles, each of these items may occur with stress, without losing their modal meaning.

Sikkert and *forresten* occur stressed postverbally with modal meaning.

(34) *Moren din   er **sikkert** sint   på deg nå.*
     mother your is surely   angry   at you now
     Your mother is mad at you now, for sure.

   Han er forresten   en ganske snill type.
   he   is by^the^way a   quite nice   guy
   By the way, he's a pretty nice guy.

Stressed *liksom* occurs as an adjectival modifier of a noun phrase, but with modal meaning.

(35) *Han er bare en **liksom** politiker.*
     he   is just a   sort^of   politician
     He is just SORT OF a politician.

Liksom may be focused without changing its modal meaning.

(36) *Han er liksom rar.*
     he   is sort^of strange
     He's sort of strange.

   Liksom ja! Han er helt   bortreist.
   sort^of yes he is completely gone^away
   Sort of! He's completely bonkers.

The Norwegian Modal Particles

Sikkert may occur as an isolated utterance with the same meaning as its modal use.

(37) *Kommer Jan på skolen idag?*
come   Jan to school today
Is Jan coming to school today?

Sikkert.
surely
Must be. *or* Most likely.

Forresten may occur sentence-initially with stress.

(38) *Forresten har jeg en god nyhet for deg.*
by^the^way have I   a   good news for you
By the way, I've got some good news for you.

All three may occur together with true modal particles, in which case the modal adverb always occurs farthest from the verb.

(39) *Vi finner nok sikkert på noe   gøy å gjøre.*
we find   MP surely on something fun to do
We're sure to find something fun to do, I suppose.

Butikken er vel forresten   stengt nå.
store   is MP by^the^way closed now
By the way, the store is closed now, isn't it?

Ole er visst liksom fars-figur   til hele bygden.
Ole is MP   sort^of father-figure to whole town
I guess Ole is sort of a father-figure to the whole town.

In summary, *sikkert, liksom,* and *forresten,* although they often occur postverbally without stress and do have a modal meaning, also occur with stress in a variety of positions, including postverbal, without losing their modal meaning. For these reasons they are not included in the class of modal particles as defined above.

1.3.3 Sentence-final usages

Many of the modal particles have sentence-final usages. Fretheim has called these "tag particles." These are stressed, although they belong to the "accent group" or phonological phrase of the immediately preceding constituents in the clause (Fretheim 1987:2). The question arises whether these should be included under the present classification of modal particles.

The modal particles *nok* and *visst* occur only postverbally. *Visstnok*, however, functions with the same meaning as *visst*, and does occur sentence finally.

(40) *Boken var visst   skrevet uten   hans tillatelse.*
     book was apparently written without his   permission
     The book was apparently written without his permission.

   Boken var skrevet uten   hans tillatelse visstnok.
   book was written without his   permission   apparently
   The book was written without his permission apparently.

In the above examples, the modal particle *visst* conveys the same idea as the tag particle *visstnok*. In spite of its lexical similarity to the modal particle *visst*, *visstnok* is clearly a modal adverb and not a modal particle, for the reasons discussed above, i.e., it may occur either stressed or unstressed in the postverbal position without losing its modal meaning. It also occurs as an isolated utterance, for example, as a one-word reply to a question.

(41) *Er det virkelig lovlig å   selge automatgevær?*
     is it   really   legal   INF sell   automatic^weapons
     Is it really legal to sell automatic weapons?

   Visstnok.
   apparently
   Apparently.

The rest of the modal particles all occur sentence finally. While in some cases the function of the tag particle may seem almost identical to that of the modal particle, in other contexts they are not substitutable for each other without a change in meaning.

Jo, as tag particle, conveys the polarity reversal of its response-particle counterpart, although at the same time suggesting that the contents of the proposition are known to the addressee (cf. §4.1.1 for a more thorough discussion of *jo* as tag particle). Henceforth, examples preceded by a text reference number, such as the following, are taken from the data corpus (cf. §3.4 and footnote one, page 51).

(42) (CA36-1)
  Du pisset ikke ut av vinduet?!
  you pissed not out of window
  You didn't piss out of the window?!

  Dassen er tett som en purk jo.
  can is clogged as a pork TAG
  Sure I did! The can is as clogged as heck!

While *vel* in postverbal position carries a subtle appeal to the listener to confirm the statement, this appeal is much stronger, almost demanding, when the particle is in sentence-final position.

(43) *Nei, vi kan vel ikke forlange at han går.*
  no we can MP not demand that he leave
  Well, I suppose we can't just demand that he leave?

  Vi kan ikke forlange at han går vel?!
  we can not demand that he leave TAG
  We can't just demand that he leave now, can we?!

Even stronger emphasis is achieved by use of the particle in both positions in the same utterance.

(44) (CA67-1)
  Hæ! Herman Hermits! Er vel ingen som går rundt med
  ha! Herman Hermits! is MP none who goes around with

  Herman Hermits på hånda vel! Med rød tusj!
  Herman Hermits on hand TAG with red felt^pen?!
  Ha! Herman Hermits! Come on! No one goes around with Herman Hermits on their hand, do they?! With a red felt pen?!

Da typically occurs as a tag particle in questions and commands, where it functions as an emphatic marker.

(45) *Få opp farten da!*
  get up speed TAG
  Get a move on!

Hva mener du nå da?
what mean you now TAG
What do you mean by that?

In assertions, it is the postverbal particle *da* which seems to carry the stronger appellative force.

(46) *Livet står   da ikke stille.*
life   stands MP not still
(You must recognize), life certainly doesn't stand still.

Livet står   ikke stille da.
life   stands not still TAG
Well, life doesn't stand still.

Another slightly different function of the tag particle *da* found in oral narrative is to signal the end of some clarifying comment or hedge, prior to resumption of the narrative.

(47) *Så kom vi til en annen landsby som fungerte som senter for hele området... en slags hovedstad da. Når vi kom dit...*
Then we came to another village that functioned as a center for the whole area... a sort of capital city (*da*). When we got there...

In conclusion, it seems that the functions of the sentence-final particle show more diversity than that of the postverbal, nonstressed particle. As shown for *da*, some of the tag particle usages closely resemble the modal particle, while others do not. For the purposes of the present study, the tag particles are distinguished from modal particles and excluded from the analysis.

1.4 Regional variety considerations

Among the approximately four million Norwegian speakers there are distinct regional differences, mostly manifested as differences in pronunciation and intonation patterns, although some lexical and syntactic differences do exist. Each major population center has its distinctive accent, and, in rural areas, differences of a few kilometers can mean identifiable differences in speech. Generally, Norwegian linguists consider major speech variety areas as relatively homogeneous, for example, referring to Southeastern Norwegian, Western Norwegian, etc.

The Norwegian Modal Particles 19

With regard to written form, the Norwegian situation is unique in that it recognizes two separate written varieties of what is basically the same language. *Bokmål* 'book Norwegian' is the written form which most closely corresponds to the speech of southeastern Norway and some larger urban areas elsewhere, which were most influenced by the Danish language during the 300 years of Danish dominance from the 1600's until the present century.

Nynorsk 'New-Norwegian' (so called because it was not standardized and recognized as an official form until relatively recently, viz. the latter part of the 19th century) is the written form which corresponds most closely to the rural varieties, especially of western and northern Norway, which were relatively less influenced by Danish than urban and southeastern speech.

In districts where both written forms have sufficient following, Norwegian school children may choose which of the two they will study as their main language, although they do receive some instruction in the other as a *sidemål* or 'side language'. It is important to remember that neither of the written forms corresponds perfectly to any of the regional speech varieties. One does not speak *Nynorsk* or *Bokmål* but a variety which may happen to be more closely represented by one of the forms than the other. However, Norwegians do not always make this distinction in everyday conversation when they may say of someone, for example, that "He speaks Nynorsk." (See Trudgill 1974 for a brief overview, and Haugen 1966 for a more complete treatment of the sociolinguistic and political implications of the Norwegian language situation.)

The data corpus used in the present study includes samples from various regional varieties of Norwegian. Although generally written in one of the two standard orthographies, spellings are often modified to indicate regional or sociolectal differences in pronunciation when representing speech (stage and radio plays, personal letters, etc.). One ramification of which the reader should be aware is that, for the text examples in this study, the modal particle *nå* will alternatively be written as *no* or *nu*, reflecting orthographic and/or regional differences. In references to the particle outside of the actual text examples, the spelling used will be *nå*.

As to the question of whether the function of a given particle may differ from one region to the next, there is no evidence that this is the case. There are, however, observable differences in frequency of occurrence of certain particles in conversation. The modal particle *nå* (Nynorsk *no*), for example, occurs more frequently in western and northern speech, while *da* (Nynorsk *då*) is more frequent in eastern Norwegian.

This brings up the interesting question of whether a given particle might be in the process of assuming the function of another particle in a given regional speech variety. This is an issue beyond the scope of the present study, although certainly a worthy topic for further research. Taking as a starting point the subtypes of function for a given particle as suggested in this paper, one might, for example, attempt to determine whether one or more of these were missing in a given variety.

While it may have been ideal to restrict the data to one homogeneous speech community (as far as this is possible) in order to not confuse functional distinctions with regional differences, the diversity of sources does not necessarily constitute a significant weakness for the present study. The Bergen variety is the aquired speech variety of the author. Being the second largest population center in Norway, Bergen's speech represents somewhat of a confluence of pure western Norwegian and the more Danish-influenced urban speech. This variety constitutes the perspective of this study: all subjective and informant-based observations are consistently made from that perspective; all textual examples used, from whatever regional source, are also in agreement with this speech variety with regard to lexical and syntactic features, including the use of modal particles.

1.5 Historical features

The Norwegian modal particles show remarkable similarity to the German modal particles, both in syntactic distribution and phonological characteristics. Both sets are typically monosyllabic, occur unstressed postverbally, and have nonmodal stressed near-homophones. Haugen (1982:5) suggests that the entire modal system was borrowed into the Scandinavian languages from Low German sometime after the Old Scandinavian period (1150–1350 A.D.).

The classes of modal particles are nearly identical in Danish, Swedish, and Norwegian with some gaps, although where found, the cognates have virtually identical function: Nynorsk *då*, Bokmål *da*, Swedish *då* and Danish *da* are equivalent; Nynorsk and Bokmål *nok*, Swedish *nog* and Danish *nok*; Nynorsk and Bokmål *vel*, Swedish *väl* and Danish *vel*; Bokmål *jo*, Swedish *ju* and Danish *jo*; and finally Swedish *dock* and Danish *dog*.

Although the system was apparently loaned from one language to another, individual items dropped out, replaced others, or merged, the resultant complexity making it difficult to trace the modal particle function of any individual item historically.

To illustrate: Old Scandinavian *tho* 'nevertheless' or 'in spite of a previous statement' (English *though*) was replaced in Swedish and Danish by the Low German *dog/dock*. This became *doch* in Modern German, which when stressed also has the meaning 'nevertheless', but when unstressed has a modal function, similar to that of Norwegian *jo*.

Norwegian *jo* and German *doch*, when stressed, both function pro-sententially as the positive answer to a negative question, as in (48).

(48) *Vil du ikke spise noe?* / *Willst du nicht etwas essen?*
      Don't you want to eat something?

   Jo. / *Doch*
   Yes (on the contrary).

Norwegian *jo*, however, lacks the stressed 'nevertheless' meaning of German *doch*. *Jo* is derived from Old Norse *jaur*, the affirmative pro-sentential particle plus an emphatic marker (de Vries 1962:291) which is related to Modern German *ja*, which interestingly also occurs as a modal particle with similar function to Norwegian *jo*.

Whether Norwegian *jo* more closely corresponds in function to German *ja* or *doch* is a question for further comparative studies. Askedal (1987) equates *jo* with *ja*, while Wesemann (1981) translates *jo* as *doch*.

2
Review of the Literature

Very little has been published on the subject of the Norwegian modal particles, and of that published there is little information on their specific semantic or pragmatic function. A wealth of literature exists, however, surrounding the historically related German modal particles, a class of lexical items which show many of the same characteristics as their Norwegian counterparts.

Because the German literature is so voluminous, it is not possible or profitable to even attempt to summarize all of it here. The purpose of the following account is to summarize some of the most ground-breaking studies of the German modal particles. In addition, some detail is recounted from German studies which have been drawn upon for the analysis of the Norwegian particles under scrutiny in this paper.

2.1 German particle research

Beginning with the pioneering works of Weydt (1969) and Krivonosov (1977, written in 1963), interest in German modal particles has increased exponentially, both in terms of theoretical studies as well as in applications to teaching of German as a second language. (Cf. Harden 1983 for an extensive annotated bibliography; also Weydt's introductory article in Weydt 1981 for a survey of modern particle-research.) According to Rösler:

> a growing interest in particles in Germany went along with a decline in interest in a sentence-oriented approach in linguistics and a general move towards pragmatics and a new interest in communication as the focus of linguistic research. (1982:33–34)

This increase in interest has culminated in a series of particle-conferences held in Berlin under the sponsorship of Harald Weydt. The first, held in September 1977, resulted in a collection of some forty papers (Weydt 1979) under such headings as particles and interaction, syntax, temporal and local phemonena, communication theory, problems of meaning, logic and argumentation, and contrastive studies (cf. Hilgendorf 1981 for a review).

The second particle-conference was held in September 1979 under the theme "Particles and German language teaching." One hundred linguists from sixteen countries convened to share research on the acquisition of particles by learners of German as a second language (cf. Schecker 1980 for a review). This particular application has been one of the strengths of the German work, and cooperation among linguists and educators has resulted in a number of helpful teaching aids, such as Weydt's (1983) *Little particle exercise book for learners of German as a foreign language* (cf. Rösler 1982 for a survey of approaches).

The third international colloquium was held in September 1982 on the function of the particle in dialogical interaction (Weydt 1983). Among the problems investigated were: whether various uses of a particle may be considered a unity or variance, and if a unity how to describe it; comparative studies with the goal of "text equivalence" rather than mere "word equivalence"; and the contribution of particles as one aspect of verbal interaction, i.e., how they work together with other elements of the utterance (Weydt 1983:1).

A fourth particle-conference was held during the summer of 1987, the results of which are not available in published form at the time of this writing, but are soon to appear (but cf. Weydt 1987 for the most up-to-date bibliography of German and other particle research available).

With this cursory overview of German particle-research as background, some of the research most significant to our present study is reviewed in greater detail. In order to understand modern research, it is helpful to backtrack to a starting point before the current interest began.

2.1.1 Particles in traditional grammar

Particles tended to be ignored in traditional German grammars. They were often regarded as unnecessary and redundant, as they made no contribution to the referential meaning of the sentence. Prescriptive grammars discouraged their use, supposing that they only indicated that the speaker was unsure of what he really wanted to say, and was trying to be vague. As a result, they were ignored in the teaching of German as a foreign language.

Much of the reason for this neglect lay in the difficulty of classifying particles within traditional grammar. Items were categorized according to their formal properties. Nouns, verbs, adjectives, etc. were distinguished by their various types of inflection for categories such as case or tense. Items which did not inflect at all were grouped together under the label of "particles." Particles in this general sense were words which had no independent lexical meaning, but rather served to contribute nuances or shades to the meanings of other words or phrases, or else to express logical or grammatical relationships.

By means of functional criteria, one could distinguish within such a class of particles such sub-sets as conjunctions, adpositions, interjections, and adverbs. By this means, modal expressions were distinguishable as those which modify not a single clausal constituent but the utterance as a whole. Arndt (1960) showed for Russian and German that by a combination of syntactic, intonational, and semantic features, such as morphological brevity, lack of intonation peak, nonelicitability or omissibility, and positional restriction, distinctions could be drawn within the class of modals between modal words, modal particles, and what he called "modal parentheses." Semantically, the modal particles were:

> additives which complement communication and ease interpretation of the message beyond its cognitive range, without themselves carrying a semantic charge. Representing, as they do, subjective shorthand signals of speaker's attitude to referent and/or interlocutor, they have some functional resemblance, not to traditional "parts of speech," but to phonemes of intonation and to gestures ... (Arndt 1960:327)

The emotional or attitudinal component was recognized by others as well. Harden (1983) cites Erben (1972) and Brinkmann (1971) as forerunners of the change in attitude. Erben characterizes "modal or emotionally expressive particles" as adding "an emotional component to the contents of an utterance." Brinkman associates modal particles with "communicative intentions and expectations." Harden sees these two definitions as an implicit recognition of modal particles as "entities which function on a level higher than the syntactic chain" (Harden 1983:17).

Schubiger (1972) brought out the parallels between German modal particles and intonation in English. She classifies the effects of the particle in a wide variety of connotations, such as protest, surprise, concession, and censure. Other usages she calls "purely emotive," such as intensifier or down-toner.

2.1.2 Modern approaches

In a work many years ahead of its time, Collinson (1938) discussed the function of the particles within the context of speech-functions and the "technique of conversation." He compares the attitudinal and emotional effects of the German particles with tag expressions and intonational devices in English.

Both Collinson and Schubiger drew upon the semantic content of the particle's stressed near-homophones, which are seen as having retained a fuller semantic content, in order to illuminate the function of the particle. This is a significant element in the present analysis of the Norwegian particles. For example, the near-homophone of *doch* is the positive answer to a negatively phrased question.

(49)   *Kommst du nicht?*
       Aren't you coming?

       Doch.
       Yes (on the contrary).

This original "adversative function" (Collinson 1938:114) is thought to be retained in the reduced modal particle *doch* which conveys the connotation "by the way you talk (or act) one would think you didn't know..." (Schubiger 1972:178).

Modern linguistics, dominated by generative grammar, showed little interest in the communicative function of particles. Only with the recent decline of sentence-oriented grammar has interest in particles again begun to pick up.

The first major work to deal exclusively with German modal particles was Krivonosov's dissertation of 1963, published in Germany in 1977. According to Krivonosov, the function of modal particles is to indicate the expressive attitude of the speaker towards the propositional contents of the utterance. This he calls "subjective modality" as opposed to the "objective modality" conveyed by modal adverbs (Krivonosov 1977:187). Thus, he views the modal particles as being combined with the predicate to form a new analytical predicate (Harden 1983:22).

Because the modal particles have no lexical meaning proper, their meaning is determined by the syntactic and situational context. Krivonosov thoroughly investigates the distribution of particles in different sentence types.

Harald Weydt, in what is recognized as one of the first major descriptive works on German modal particles, recognized two levels of language. On one hand is the "representational level" (*Darstellungsebene*). On this level, a given state of affairs is specified, fixed in time and space, and given reference in the real world. Modality on this level reflects the speaker's assessment of this state of affairs, its certainty, its desirability, and to what degree it may be expected or regarded as surprising. Such modals would include the modal adverbs.

On the other hand is the "intentional level" (*Intentionsebene*). This level shows the attitude of the speaker toward the utterance. This is shown in all languages through the physical context, nonverbal cues, pitch height, accent, intonation, rate of speech, volume, and word order.

According to Weydt (1969:60), "By means of these signs, the hearer recognizes whether the speaker is excited about what he is saying, whether he is bored, in doubt, convinced, whether he expects a 'yes' or 'no' answer, etc." The intentional level involves an "assessment of the assessment" (*ein Urteil über das Urteil*). It is on this level that the modal particles (Weydt called them shading particles—*Abtönungspartikeln*) belong. Weydt thus makes the same distinction as Krivonosov's objective vs. subjective modality, calling them ADVERB MODALITY, and SHADING MODALITY respectively:

> Adverb modality and shading modality differ in that the adverb belongs to the assessment, while the shading to the assessment of the assessment. (Weydt 1969:64, my translation)

Thus a qualitative distinction is made between modal particles and other expressions of modality, the modal particles belonging somehow to a higher plane of communication more analagous to intonation and prosodic features than to lexical expressions. This discussion is taken up again in chapter five, with regard to the unique function of modal particles in relation to their distinctive formal properties.

Lütten's research (1977, 1979) was set in the framework of speech-act theory. Her goal was to discover the communicative role of the particles, something for which morphological and syntactical analysis had proven inadequate. The analysis was based on textual data, specifically "discussions" or "argumentation," in which speakers present evidence in an attempt to make the others accept their opinions. Lütten postulates that speakers use particles to help secure the acceptance of their statements by referring to some common basis shared by speaker and addressee.

While particles on the whole make recourse to some common basis, the particles *doch, eben,* and *ja* in particular accomplish this by constituting a "consensus."

> In all three cases an appeal to a communicative mutuality is present. The mutuality consists of the following: that two or more persons hold the "same" view, have had the "same" experience, seen or heard the "same" fact or event. An important element is that the formation of this mutuality is necessary for the advancement of the argumentation. (Lütten 1977:270, my translation)

For example, the phrase *Es ist ja wahr, daß* 'It is true that' with the particle *ja*, makes the assumption that it is general knowledge, and already accepted by speaker and addressee that 'it is true'. If the addressee does not protest immediately, the speaker is free to proceed as if this were an accepted given, and thus gains an advantage over his interlocuter. The same statement without the particles makes no such assumption, but merely offers the naked assertion 'it is true that', which then must be accepted before the speaker can proceed to build further arguments upon it.

The value of the particle in argumentation is in "representing the basis of what one is advocating as generally known and recognized, whether it actually is or not." The particle "allows the possibility of actualizing norms and of presenting them as accepted and affirmed without at the same time thematizing and problematizing them" (Lütten 1977:246–7, my translation). Statements which otherwise might be subjected to controversy may be presented as if generally accepted, and thus the argument is free to proceed on the basis of these statements. Lütten goes so far as to say that this establishing of a consensus is one of the universal characteristics of human communication.

The analysis of each particle consists of comparing the modal particle with each of its other uses and near-homophones. Lütten postulates that lexical items with logical meaning develop usages whereby the logical form of the utterance is not affected. These are their particle usages. What has taken place is a "semantic reduction" which results in a weakening of the primary function of the item (Lütten 1977:232).

Doch, for example, originated as a one-word sentence. It expresses contrast between a positive answer to a negatively phrased question or statement. This continues to be the meaning of its form when stressed or in isolation. While this use may appear at first glance to have nothing in common with the "recourse-to-a-common-basis" function of the particle, Lütten claims that by semantic analysis, certain properties common to both the stressed or isolated form and the semantically reduced particle can be discovered.

Though one might wish to say that *doch* with stress expresses contrast, but *doch* without stress refers to a common basis, this difference cannot be maintained. The fact that a speaker, by means of the utterance *Du bist doch dumm* refers to a common basis, shows that they, at the moment of the utterance, are apparently disturbed that an assertion or presumption has been made which stands in opposition to what can be presupposed as known and recognized. On the basis of these considerations, the oppositional structure of *doch* may be established. (Lütten 1977:245, my translation)

Taking into account elements of meaning present in the near-homophones, and relating these to the particle usage allows Lütten to discern various shades of function within the set of "consensus-constitutive" particles *doch*, *eben*, and *ja*. *Doch* suggests a situation in which the speaker appeals to the addressee to call to memory something which he is quite aware of. *Eben* calls upon the addressee to recognize the factuality of some state of affairs as necessary and unavoidable, and to take the consequences. *Ja* presents a fact or opinion as certain. Of the three, *ja* makes the clearest recourse to a common basis.

Bublitz (1978) treated modal particles in the larger context of his investigation of various means of expression of speaker's attitudes. He compares and contrasts means of attitude expression in German and English. Modal particles are just one means of expressing speaker attitude in German. Although English does not have modal particles, speaker attitudes are expressed by means of tags, intonation, stress patterns, and sentence types, although there is not necessarily one-to-one correspondence of these expressions from German to English.

Bublitz calls the speaker's attitude EMOTIVE MODALITY, drawing on distinctions made by Bühler (1934) and Jakobson (1960) between the cognitive or denotative content of an utterance, and the speaker's emotive or conative assessment of the utterance. Bublitz recognized three types of modality, the COGNITIVE, the VOLITIVE, and the EMOTIVE.

Cognitive modality refers to:

> the attitude toward the content of an utterance... when the speaker comments on the truth-content of the proposition, and makes known whether he evaluates the relationship between subject and predicate... as valid, invalid, probably valid, etc. (Bublitz 1978:7, my translation)

Volitive modality refers to the speaker's wish or will to influence the behavior of the addressee, or to change an act or a situation.

The third kind of modality, emotive modality, is described as the speaker's use of language when he

> conveys his assumptions and attitudes in relation to the common underlying knowledge of his communication partner, his expectations and emotions, and their mutual social relationship to each other. (Bublitz 1978:8, my translation)

Both modal particles and modal words belong to this emotive-conative means of expression, but modal words are shown to differ morphologically, syntactically, and semantically from modal particles (cf. §1.3.1). Modal words may belong to the cognitive modality and thus affect the truth value of a proposition, while modal particles are always expressions of emotive modality.

The theoretical framework within which Bublitz' analysis is carried out is that of conversation analysis, based on Grice's conversational maxims and implicatures. The data corpus consists of novels with dialogue. By looking at the larger structure of conversations, the conversational implicature of an individual particle is determined.

For example, the modal particle *ja* signals a breach of Grice's maxim of Quantity (cf. §3.1) by stating something already familiar to the addressee. The fact that this maxim has been breached further implies that the speaker has some good reason for doing so (Bublitz 1978:96).

The implicatures carried by the particle *ja* in the German sentence X = *Wir gehen ja nie aus dem Haus* 'We never do go out of the house' may be described as follows:

1. X is known.
2. The speaker wants to establish that X actually belongs to the common base of knowledge.
3. The speaker wants to certify that X is equally valid for the addressee.

In Grice's terms, number one above is known as a conventional implicature, that is, an inference attached by convention to particular lexical items or expressions (Levinson 1983:127). Numbers two and three are known as conversational implicatures, those inferences derived from the content plus some specific assumptions about the cooperative nature of ordinary verbal interaction (Levinson 1983:104).

Franck (1980) carried out her research in a theoretical framework which combined speech-act theory and conversation analysis. Acknowledging that the classic categories of speech-act theory only illuminate a portion of the aspects of particle meaning, she sets up a "check-list" of conditions under which a given particle may occur, with which to evaluate its "potential aspects of meaning." The conditions are divided into four categories according to which of the various "factors of communication" they relate to.

The "conversational conditions" relate to the structure of sequences of exchanges in dialogue, such as the nature of preceding and following turns, and the nature of the turn containing the particle, whether initiative, reactive, or both.

The second category refers to the modification effected by the particle upon the particle utterance itself. This includes epistemic qualification of the proposition, or modification of the illocutive force of the utterance.

The third category of conditions relates to the interactional context—the speech situation as it involves speaker and addressee, their social relationship and status, and the effect of the utterance, whether cooperative, challenging, or something else.

The final category involves "interpretational factors," such as reference to Grice's maxims of conversation, or "interpretational strategies" whether the utterance is to be understood literally, ironically, rhetorically, or idiomatically (Franck 1980:169–170).

Franck addresses the question of what are the context-free, inherent aspects of meaning versus those which are context-dependent implicatures. The issue is problematic because of the difficulty of describing contextual factors in the abstract. Many of the implicatures blocked or triggered by the particle are of such a general nature, i.e., they apply to so many contexts, that they approach permanent meaning (Franck 1980:167).

Baunebjerg and Wesemann (1983) would apply Frank's checklist toward the development of a "descriptive catalogue" of particle features, with the eventual goal of a particle dictionary listing monolingual entries along with their translation equivalents (cf. Bastert 1985 for a similar attempt with *doch*). The question of which features are basic and which are derived from these is ignored here.

The results of the analysis of Baunebjerg and Wesemann are given in this short article only for German *schon* and Danish *nok*. Several aspects of Franck's CONVERSATIONAL, CONTENT, and INTERACTIONAL components of particle meaning are listed (Franck's interpretational category has apparently been fused with the interactional), and findings pertaining to both *schon* and *nok* are listed. From Baunebjerg and Weseman's presentation it appears that they regard the two particles as equivalent with regard to each of the factors listed. It is not clear whether they intend the description to represent merely the least common denominator of the functions of the two particles, or whether they actually consider them entirely equal in function, something which would seem unlikely.

Given the close relationship between Danish and Norwegian, the comparative Danish/German particle studies done by Baunebjerg and Weseman with regard to their specific conclusions about individual particles have the greatest impact on Norwegian particle analysis of any works reviewed here. Both of them approach their studies within the framework of German particle-analysis represented by the Berlin particle-colloquiums.

Baunebjerg (1979) examines Danish equivalents to German *genau, gerade,* and *eben* in various functions as answering particles, temporal adverbs, adjective-adverbs, and finally as modal particles or degree particles. In differentiating modal from degree particles, she shows that the same syntactic criteria can be used for Danish as for German. While the general "emotional-communicative" function of indicating speaker's attitude towards the utterance is the same, the particular nuances of attitude conveyed by a correspondence pair are not equivalent in all sentence types. Thus, a direct translation is not always possible.

Wesemann's article (in Weydt 1981) investigates Danish equivalents to German *doch* in declarative, interrogative, and exclamatory sentences. She notes that *doch* may sometimes be translated by *jo* and sometimes by *da*. Drawing on Lütten's notion of an "appellative recourse to a common basis of communication," she hypothesizes three elements of meaning conveyed by *doch* in the utterance *Sie kennen mich doch nicht* 'You don't know me':

(50) Proposition:
      'You don't know me.'

      Recourse to a common base of knowledge:
      'You are already aware that you don't know me.'

      Appeal:
      'Please acknowledge that you don't know me.'

She then explains the difference in function between *jo* and *da* by claiming that *da* contains all three of the above elements, while *jo* contains only the first two and lacks the appellative element.

As evidence for this, she shows that *jo*, but not *da*, may be used in reported conversation, such as indirect quotation of speech or thoughts (*indirekten Rede* 'indirect conversation' or *erlebten Rede* 'experienced conversation'):

(51) *Daniela bleibt stehen vor Verwunderung darüber, daß sie so etwas denkt. Sie braucht ihn **doch** nicht. Wozu auch.*
Daniela kept wondering how she could think this way. After all, she didn't (*doch*) need him. What would she use him for?

This may be translated using *jo*:

(52) *Hun behøver ham **jo** ikke. Hvad skulle hun også bruge ham til?*
She didn't (*jo*) need him. What would she use him for?

She shows that the particle *da*, however, may not appear in indirect conversation in this context, as in (53), because it implies a direct appeal by the speaker to his interlocutor (Wesemann 1981:240–1).

(53) *Hun behøver ham da ikke.*
She didn't (*da*) need him.

2.2 Other modal particle research

While the German work is significant by virtue of the close relationship to the Scandinavian languages, other relevant observations have been made about modal systems of similar function in unrelated languages.

Kuno (1973:5) described a class of sentence-final particles in Japanese which indicate "the speaker's attitude to the content of the sentence" (=p) as follows:

(54) yo 'I am telling you that p.'
      ne 'I hope you agree that p.'
      ka 'I ask you if p.'
      sa 'It goes without saying that p.'

These appear to consist of modifications of the speech act or illocutionary force of the utterance.

Likewise Donaldson's set of "belief clitics" in Ngiyambaa would appear to be just as much discourse as modal features:

Assertion: "used to draw the addressee's attention to a statement."

Categorical assertion: "the speaker presents the statement... as significant for its absolute truth."

Counter-assertion: "Either contradicts a previous statement or is intended to counter some presupposition the speaker suspects his addressee of entertaining."

Hypothesis: "Marks a statement as an unconfirmed hypothesis on the part of the speaker." (Donaldson 1980:252–5)

Mandarin Chinese, according to Li and Thompson, has a system of sentence-final particles with elusive semantic and pragmatic functions, which are found "in speech or in writings that reflect or recount conversations." In a striking parallel to the Scandinavian and German modal particles, these are phonologically reduced (unstressed and with neutral tone), and they occur in other contexts serving different functions, evidence of their having undergone a semantic reduction process similar to the one postulated below for the Norwegian modal particles. Their "basic communicative functions" are summarized by Li and Thompson (1981:238ff) as follows:

(55) le   'currently relevant state'
      ne   'response to expectation'
      ba   'solicit agreement'
      ou   'friendly warning'
      a/ya   'reduce forcefulness'
      ma   'question'

While systems such as those described here are often treated under the label of modal systems, there is no strict agreement on what should be included under the term MODALITY. Emotions, subjective attitudes and opinions of the speaker, speech acts and illocutionary force, discourse, and pragmatic features are all among the general phenomena covered by the broad concept of modality.

Palmer acknowledges that "much of modal meaning is included in what is sometimes distinguished as 'pragmatics'" (Palmer 1986:3). At the same time he "links discourse ... closely to modality, for speaker attitudes are often related to known facts, derived from both the linguistic and the nonlinguistic situation" (Palmer 1986:34). Thus, it is surprising, but perhaps some indication of the confusion around the term MODALITY, when he comments on the German modal particles that "these all seem to be essentially comments on the proposition rather than opinions about it, and so not very obviously modal" (Palmer 1986:46). The distinction here is not at all clear. Palmer fails to say what the particles should be called, if they are not modal.

3
Theoretical Framework

Although there exists no consensus on precisely how the study of pragmatics should be defined, simply stated, pragmatics refers to the study of language use. It may be distinguished from semantics, the study of meaning, and syntax, the study of words in combination. The relationship between these three fields of inquiry was first distinguished by the philosopher Charles Morris as follows: syntax involves the relation of signs to one another, semantics the relations of signs to their referents, while pragmatics refers to the relation of signs to their interpreters (Levinson 1983:1).

Pragmatic study distinguishes itself from syntax and semantics in that it is a more recent area of interest, and thus offers a less developed methodology. What is meant by the term PRAGMATIC ANALYSIS is not a strict application of some rigorous theoretical or notational framework, but rather an investigation wherein aspects of meaning not covered by propositional semantics are to be explored. This is especially suited to the phenomenon of the modal particles, precisely because much of modality, as suggested in the previous chapter, lies outside the realm of truth-conditional semantics.

Among various approaches which may be called pragmatic approaches, there are three recent theoretical or methodological frameworks which have proven fruitful in the analysis of modal particles, and whose concepts and constructs have been utilized in the present analysis of Norwegian modal particles. These are briefly outlined here.

3.1 Grice's theory of implicature

3.1.1 Conversational implicatures

The concept of implicature is grounded in the observation that, in human language, what a given utterance means is often more than what is actually said. Consider the following exchange:

(56)   A: Have you seen Joe?
       B: There's a blue Mazda outside Mary's house.

The literal semantic meaning of B's utterance would in no way qualify as an answer to A's question. A inquires as to whether or not B has seen a certain individual, and B states that a certain type of car is located outside another individual's house—on the surface, two completely unrelated utterances.

In ordinary conversation, however, B's reply would be understood as a perfectly normal response. B understands that A is not interested in whether B has seen Joe but actually wants to know Joe's whereabouts. B then communicates that no, he is not able to provide the information with certainty, but he does have some information which may be useful to A in locating him, namely that a type of car which Joe is known to drive is located outside Mary's house, and so therefore it is likely that Joe is visiting Mary. The real communication in this exchange consists not in the literal semantic meaning of the expressions, but in what is inferred. As Levinson summarizes,

> inferences are fundamental to our sense of coherence in discourse: if the implicatures were not constructed on the basis of the assumption of relevance, many adjacent utterances in conversation would appear quite unconnected. (Levinson 1983:107)

"Conversational implicatures," as Grice (1975) called them, are derived because there is a principle to which speakers adhere, and to which they assume their interlocutor adheres in normal conversation. This assumption of cooperation, together with the specific speech situation plus the literal semantic interpretation of the utterance, gives rise to certain implicatures, which are included in the total meaning, or communicative intent of the speaker.

Grice called this principle the "cooperative principle," which he defined as follows:

Theoretical Framework

Make your conversational contribution such as is required, at the stage at which it occurs, by the accepted purpose or direction of the talk exchange in which you are engaged. (Grice 1975:45)

Under this general principle he distinguished four specific "maxims of conversation" which speakers follow in order to comply with the cooperative principle. These he termed the maxims of quantity, quality, relation, and manner (Grice 1975:45–46).

QUANTITY

1. Make your contribution as informative as is required (for the current purposes of the exchange).
2. Do not make your contribution more informative than is required.

QUALITY. Try to make your contribution one that is true.

1. Do not say what you believe to be false.
2. Do not say that for which you lack adequate evidence.

RELATION. Be relevant.

MANNER. Be perspicuous.

1. Avoid obscurity of expression.
2. Avoid ambiguity.
3. Be brief.
4. Be orderly.

The point is that, faced with any utterance, even one which lacks a readily interpretable literal meaning, the hearer will attribute to it some interpretation as if it conformed to the maxims. For example, in the exchange in (56), speaker A will assume that B is conforming to the cooperative principle, specifically the maxim of RELATION, by making his reply relevant to the question. Speaker A will thus make a search, utilizing contextual factors as well as the literal meaning of the utterance, in order to give B's utterance some interpretation which can be construed as a cooperative reply.

While Grice showed that certain implicatures are derived from his maxims of quantity, quality, relation, and manner, there may be other maxims or principles of interaction which give rise to different types of implicatures. Atlas and Levinson (1981) postulate a "principle of informativeness" which creates implicatures sometimes in conflict with those created by the maxim of QUANTITY. R. Lakoff (1973b) suggests a set of "politeness rules" which operate side by side with the other conversational maxims. In a recent work, Sperber and Wilson (1982, 1986), argue that implicatures may be deduced from a single overriding principle of RELEVANCE which would thus obsolete Grice's maxims.

3.1.2 Particles as hedges on conversational maxims

Although the notion of conversational implicature refers to language use, it may have implications for, and thus be essential to, the description of certain morphological and syntactic structures. The function of certain grammatical morphemes and lexical items may be to modify conversational maxims, that is, to indicate just how an utterance containing them lives up to cooperative expectations (Levinson 1983:162).

English expressions like *well, oh, ah, so, anyway, actually, still, after all, by the way, now, all right, you know* have been shown to function as HEDGES on conversational maxims (R. Lakoff 1973a, James 1972, 1973). See Baker 1975 for other English expressions as maxim hedges, and Brown and Levinson 1978 for extensive examples in other languages; also cf. G. Lakoff for elaboration on the hedge concept. Brown and Levinson define HEDGE as:

> a particle, word, or phrase that modifies the degree of membership of a predicate or noun phrase in a set; it says of that membership that it is *partial*, or true only in certain respects, or that it is *more* true and complete than perhaps might be expected (note that this latter sense is an extension of the colloquial sense of 'hedge'). (1978:150)

For example, the English particle *well* may function as a hedge on the quantity maxim, indicating that the utterance does not supply all of the information requested (R. Lakoff 1973a), as in the following exchange:

(57) A: What time is it?
     B: Well, the sun just came up.

Schubiger (1972) showed that hedging in German is partially accomplished by modal particles. This would appear to be true in Norwegian as well. Brown and Levinson (1978:169) give examples of quality hedges which "suggest that the speaker is not taking full responsibility for the truth of his utterance," such as in (58).

Theoretical Framework

(58) I think...
      I believe...
      I suppose...

The Norwegian modal particles *nok, vel,* and *visst* would appear to have similar function. Other quality hedges may "disclaim the assumption that the point of S's assertion is to inform H" (Brown and Levinson 1978:170), such as:

(59) As you know...
      As is well known...
      As you and I both know...

As will be seen below, Norwegian *jo* offers a similar disclaimer.

3.2 Speech act theory

3.2.1 Truth conditions

In his series of lectures published posthumously in 1962 as "How to do things with words," J. L. Austin went against the assumptions of his time that meaningful utterances must be understood according to their TRUTH CONDITIONS, or those conditions which must obtain in order for them to be true. He examined a class of sentences which are true by virtue of their being uttered:

(60) I dub you Sir William Longbottom.
      I promise to be there Friday.
      I apologize for insulting you.

Rather than just saying things, these sentences do things. Austin called these PERFORMATIVES, as opposed to CONSTATIVES, which make a statement about the world. Performatives are not evaluated according to whether they are true or false, but rather whether they are successful or unsuccessful, as determined by whether they conform to certain conditions, which he called FELICITY CONDITIONS. For example, the first statement above may be successfully uttered only if the speaker has the position of authority required to confer such a title, the second only if the speaker intends to come on Friday, and so on.

As his argument evolves, however, Austin proceeds to show that constatives are also performatives in that they do things, albeit a special subclass of indirect performatives wherein the act being performed is not explicitly stated. A statement like "The world is round" is a speech act, or ILLOCUTIONARY ACT, implicitly equivalent to "I assert that the world is round." The statement is said to have the illocutionary force of an assertion (Austin 1962).

Searle (1969, 1975, 1976) further codified and systematized Austin's speech act theory. For him, the felicity conditions are more than just conditions for the success of an utterance. They actually constitute the various illocutionary forces. Where Austin classified performative utterances according to performative verbs such as *agree*, *promise*, *deny*, Searle developed a classification based on the felicity conditions themselves.

Four basic types of felicity conditions are postulated. First, there are conditions on the PROPOSITIONAL CONTENT of the utterance. In promising, for example, speaker S must be predicating a future act A to be done by himself. PREPARATORY CONDITIONS are those which, although they do not constitute the essential feature, are necessary for the act to be performed, for example, that S believes that H would prefer his doing A to his not doing A. SINCERITY CONDITIONS require that S truly intends to do the act promised. Finally, the ESSENTIAL CONDITION is that S, in uttering the promise, actually undertakes an obligation to perform A (Searle 1969:57-60). Cf. also Searle, Kieter and Bierwisch 1980, Cole and Morgan 1975, and Bach and Harnish 1979 for further introduction to speech act theory; Edmondson 1981, Klammer 1971, 1973, and Longacre 1983 for alternative models.

3.2.2 Particles as hedges on illocutionary force

Hedges on illocutionary force, or PERFORMATIVE HEDGES, modify the illocutionary force of an utterance. One way to analyze such hedges is as adverbs modifying implied performative verbs which represent the illocutionary force of the sentence (Corum 1974, Fraser 1975). A sentence such as (61) could be represented as (62).

(61)   Won't you open the door?

(62)   I hedgedly request that you open the door.   (G. Lakoff 1972:213)

Other studies have shown that performative hedges modify illocutionary force by strengthening or weakening the felicity conditions associated with

Theoretical Framework

a given illocutionary act. R. Lakoff (1972, following Uyeno 1971) claims that the Japanese particle *ne* suspends the sincerity condition on assertions, the preparatory condition on orders, and the essential condition on questions. Brown and Levinson (1978) give examples of Tzeltal particles which act as illocutionary force hedges. The dubitative particle *mak*, for example, suspends the felicity condition on assertions that the speaker knows what he says to be true, in some cases turning a statement into more of a question. The English equivalent would make use of sentence-final tags such as 'I suppose' or 'I guess' (Brown and Levinson 1978:159). The Norwegian modal particle *vel* appears to have a similar function.

Any overlap between the types of hedges presented above is not coincidental. Work since the time of Austin has related the concept of illocutionary force to Grice's theory of communication. It is, after all, the principles of cooperation in conversation which determine conditions for the successful utterance of different speech acts. The QUALITY maxim is realized as sincerity conditions, the RELEVANCE maxim as preparatory conditions, and so forth. What the hedges ultimately do, is to "emphasize that the cooperative condition is met, or serve notice that it may not have been met, or question whether it has been met" (Brown and Levinson 1978:169).

3.3 Conversation analysis

In recent years the realization has grown that illocutionary force may be best studied and understood, not in sentences in isolation, but in the larger context of conversation. CONVERSATION ANALYSIS (CA) has shown that the functions performed by utterances are largely determined by the place they occupy within certain interactional sequences. The transition from speech act theory to conversation analysis was well summarized by Atkinson and Heritage.

> The development of speech act theory...in linguistics has greatly forwarded the view that utterances can be usefully analyzed as conventionally grounded social actions. However, this viewpoint has developed within a disciplinary matrix which gives analytic primacy to the isolated sentence... This mode of analysis has been the object of sustained criticism within the literature of conversation analysis... [where] utterances are *in the first instance* contextually understood by reference to their placement and participation within sequences of actions. For conversation analysts, therefore, it is sequences and turns within sequences,

rather than isolated sentences or utterances, that have become the primary units of analysis. (Atkinson and Heritage 1984:5, emphasis theirs)

First developed by sociologists, CA has been established as an independent field of study (cf. Sacks, Schegloff and Jefferson 1974, Schegloff and Sacks 1973, Schegloff 1984). The goal of analysis is a functional account of conversational structures. Explanations are sought in terms of interactional strategies employed by speakers and manifested by certain structural clues.

The unique advantage of conversation as opposed to monologue texts as an object of linguistic study is that, in conversation, each utterance contains within it an analysis of the other speaker's previous utterance. CA methodology involves the observation of recurring structural patterns in conversational data in order to form hypotheses regarding speakers' sequential expectations and their orientation to these expectations.

CA is a rigorously empirical means of investigation which approaches the data with few if any preconceived theoretical constructs. Above all, it marks a determined departure from traditional methods of analysis based on the speaker's intuition or observer's field notes. Naturally occurring conversational data collected by audio or video recording equipment is favored for the diversity of its structural features. Pauses, hesitations, and interruptions, as well as pitch, volume, and other prosodic cues are considered important to the analysis, and usually included to the degree possible in transcriptions of the recorded data. (Cf. Heritage 1984 for an illustrative application of CA theory to the English particle *oh;* also Owen 1981, 1983 and Carlson 1984 on English *well.*)

3.4 Data corpus

While it may be true to say that speech act theory has been superseded by the techniques of conversation analysis, this is not the same as to say it is obsolete. It is not necessary to abandon all of the concepts of the former in order to utilize the insights of the latter where the two are not in conflict. An eclectic approach has been taken in the present study which makes use of both empirical sequential analysis as well as speaker's intuitions and contrived examples along with conversational data.

Just as the present analysis does not rely exclusively on the methodology and concepts of conversation analysis, neither does it adhere to its strict constraints on acceptable data. Where most CA researchers would insist upon more or less detailed transcriptions of naturally occurring conversation,

Theoretical Framework

including hesitations, pauses, and false starts (and the degree of detail is by no means agreed upon, cf. Levinson 1983:295–6), the corpus which forms the basis for the present study consists of written texts of several radio and stage plays as well as personal letters.

Two objections might arise here. One, the transcriptions lack the detail of prosodic and other features typically included in CA transcriptions, features which undeniably often have some pragmatic significance. Secondly, the complaint might be made that such data is not "naturally occurring conversational data" and is therefore not suitable as the object of linguistic study.

To begin with, the first objection need not be perceived as a weakness when we consider that the goal of the present analysis is not to account for any and all structural features of sequential exchanges which may be relevant to particle usage, but rather to identify the central elements of the function of particles in relation to speaker strategy.

An analysis of particle usage in relation to hesitations, false starts, pitch, and intonational features would doubtless be an interesting study. But that is not the focus of the present research. Perhaps it would not be unreasonable to say that even though such detail is not available, the most significant clues to speakers' interactional strategies are the actual lexical and syntactic expressions chosen. These are, of course, still available in the present data corpus.

Further, while acknowledging that some features are lost in a regularized corpus, certain prosodic cues are still available, as indicated by means of punctuation, boldface type and italics, and various stage directions. These at least indicate the functions of various intonation, stress, volume, and pitch patterns.

As for the second objection that radio and stage plays are not a record of "naturally occurring" conversation, neither can these be labelled as data contrived for the purpose of the analysis. Such texts are natural, "real" data in the sense that they have been produced by a native speaker (albeit only one instead of two or more) in accordance with his native speaker competence. That such data is rich with particles suggests that sufficient grounds for the presence and choice of particles are present in the context and therefore likely to be accessible to the analyst.

Baunebjerg and Wesemann, in fact, claim that written texts offer a better basis for the observation of particle function because in written texts particles are often the only means by which attitudes can be conveyed which, in spoken language, might be indicated by intonation, gestures, or tone of voice (Baunebjerg and Wesemann 1983:120).

4
A Functional Analysis of *jo* and *nå*

4.1 *Jo*

4.1.1 Reduction from *jo* as response particle

Before considering the modal particle *jo* in its various usages, it will be helpful to discuss the relationship between *jo*, as modal particle, and its stressed near-homophone *jo* as a response particle (or "sentence-equivalent" particle as often called in the German literature, cf. Lütten 1977:242 and others). The relevance of this will be evident. If we can show that the modal particle was derived by phonological and semantic reduction from stressed *jo*, then we might expect the reduced form to have retained some elements of meaning of the nonreduced form. In other words, the meaning of stressed *jo* may be drawn upon for clues as to the function of the modal particle *jo*.

As with most languages, Norwegian has response particles roughly equivalent to English *yes* and *no*. In answer to assertions or questions phrased in the positive (with positive polarity, cf. Van Valin 1975:625), *ja* expresses agreement and *nei* disagreement. In response to assertions or questions with negative polarity, however, they both convey agreement.

(63) A: *Det går ikke an.*
      that goes not on
      That's not possible.

   B: *Nei, det gjør ikke det.*
      no it does not that
      No, it isn't.

45

or:

    B: *Ja, der har du rett.*
       yes there have you right
       Yes, you're right about that.

Each of B's responses above indicate agreement with A. In order to convey disagreement, *jo* must be used.

(64) A: *Det går ikke an.*
         the goes not on.
         That's not possible.

      B: *Jo.*   *Det gjør det.*
         on^the^contrary that does it
         Yes it is.

Whereas the response particles *ja* and *nei* maintain the polarity of the previous utterance, *jo* constitutes a polarity reversal, or contrast between the negative stance of the previous utterance and the positive reply.

A distinction must be made between negative polarity and a negative expectation. While *jo* reverses the negative polarity of a previous utterance, it may or may not reverse the expectation which it signals. In the following exchange, where speaker A expects a negative reply, the polarity reversal of the reply goes against this expectation:

(65) A: *Du kommer ikke til festen gjør du?*
         you come not to party do you
         You're not coming to the party, are you?

      B: *Jo.*
         on^the^contrary
         Yes, I am.

However, where the question is phrased in the negative, albeit with the expectation of a positive reply, the polarity reversal counters only the negative stance of the question, and not the expectation.

(66) A: *Du kommer til festen, ikke sant?*
         you come to party not true
         You're coming to the party, right?

A Functional Analysis of *jo* and *nå*　　　　　　　　　　　　　　47

  B: *Jo.*
    on^the^contrary
    That's right.

Stressed *jo* may constitute the entire reply. More commonly, however, it is accompanied by another utterance which expands upon the simple polarity reversal.

(67) A: *Du har ikke vasket deg på mange uker!*
    you have not washed REFL in many weeks
    You haven't washed for many weeks!

   B: *Jo, det har jeg. Jeg vasker meg hver dag.*
    yes that have I　I wash REFL every day
    Yes I have. I wash every day.

Perhaps the most common type of utterance to occur as the expansion of a *jo* response is one which gives some kind of support for the polarity reversal, often in the form of a GROUNDS proposition.

(68) A: *Du pisset ikke ut av vinduet?!*
    you pissed not out of window
    You didn't piss out of the window?!

   B: *Jo. Dassen er tett som en purk.*
    yes can is clogged as a pork
    Yeah I did. The can is clogged as heck.

Recall the sentence-final tag particles from §1.3.3 above. These occur with stress, as part of the immediately preceding phonological phrase. We concluded that these have functions distinct from the unstressed, postverbal modal particles, and should therefore not be included in the class of modal particles. The tag particle *jo* was seen to have the polarity-reversing function of stressed *jo*.

(69) A: *Du pisset ikke ut av vinduet?!*
    you pissed not out of window
    You didn't piss out of the window?!

B: *Dassen er tett   som en purk jo!*
   can   is clogged as a pork TAG
   Sure I did! The can is clogged as heck!

While the primary effect of the tag particle above is to reverse the polarity of A's utterance, there is also an element of censure, as if B thinks the answer should already be obvious to A, and thus is criticizing A for asking a needless question. This censure is not present in the example before, where B merely answers with the response particle *jo* followed by an explanation. Semantically, the tag particle seems to lie somewhere between the polarity reversal of the response particle and the PROPOSITION AS KNOWN effect of the modal particle.

Note also that the tag particle has been partially integrated into the grounds proposition structurally. While the response particle could occur alone or sentence initially followed by a pause, the tag particle must belong to the same phonological phrase as the immediately preceding constituent. It may not be separated from the grounds proposition by a pause. The modal particle, however, is even further integrated into the grounds proposition, occurring only postverbally.

(70) A: *Du pisset ikke ut   av vinduet?!*
       you pissed not out of window
       You didn't piss out of the window?!

   B: *Dassen er jo tett   som en purk!*
      can   is MP clogged as a pork
      Well the can is clogged as heck you know!

What we appear to have is a progression from response particle to modal particle, involving the incorporation of the polarity reversal into the grounds proposition. The tag particle is the missing link as it were, showing the semantic connection between *jo* as an independant utterance, and *jo* as modal particle.

This progression takes place on two levels. First of all, the particle is progressively reduced phonologically. In the first example, *jo* is stressed and may be separated from the grounds proposition by an intervening pause of indefinite length. Where *jo* occurs sentence finally, although still stressed, it must belong to the same phonological phrase as the preceding grounds proposition, i.e., it may have no pause preceding it. This represents the first stage of phonological reduction. Finally, where it occurs postverbally, the particle cannot take stress, and has been fully cliticized to the verb. This represents the most phonologically reduced stage.

A progression has taken place at the semantic level as well. As the particle is incorporated into the grounds proposition, the element of polarity reversal becomes increasingly less dominant, while the grounds proposition becomes more so.

But now we must answer the question of how the modal particle came to signal that the proposition containing it is already known by the addressee. The function of a grounds proposition is analogous to that of a given in a logical deductive argument of the form:

(71)   given that x
          if y
       _____
          then z

The given proposition is a statement which is presupposed or on which consensus already exists, and which may therefore be built upon for the purpose of drawing a deductive conclusion upon which consensus does NOT exist. If a given is used which is not beyond question, then, in order for it to be effective in the advancement of the conclusion, another argument must first be resolved as to the truth or falsity of the given. So the important and most salient feature of a given is that it states a proposition upon which consensus exists. Likewise the dominant feature of a grounds proposition is that it contains information upon which consensus exists between speaker and hearer.

Thus it appears that, in becoming integrated with a grounds proposition, *jo* as modal particle has taken on the dominant feature of the proposition with which it was fused, conveying the implicature that recourse is being made to a proposition upon which consensus exists.

As for the polarity-reversal element present in stressed *jo*, what we will see below is that there are instances where both polarity reversal and recourse to consensus clearly are conveyed by the *jo* proposition. In other cases the polarity reversal is not as evident. Whether or not polarity reversal is present in such cases is discussed in §§4.1.7 and 4.1.8.

4.1.2 The basic meaning of MP *jo*

At first glance, the obvious basic feature of the *jo* particle is that it conveys that the information contained in the utterance is somehow already known to the addressee. There are indications that modal expressions involving common access to information between speaker and addressee may be fairly common—there are several other languages which have particles with very similar functions. Van Valin (1975:636) lists several, quoting from various sources. According to Wolff, the Indonesian particle *dong* expresses the attitude of the speaker that the addressee should be aware of the facts being stated. Boas and Deloria show for Lakhota that the sentence-final particle *was* implies "that a question is unnecessary, that the questioner ought to know the answer." The Russian particle *ved*, according to Vasilyeva, emphasizes that a fact contained in an utterance is obvious. The statement merely reminds the hearer of something he already knows. Finally, Van Valin quotes Zimmer, who claims that the Turkish sentence-final particle *ki* "expresses the attitude of the speaker that the hearer should have already known what he is telling him." Also according to Hensarling (1982), Kogi, a language of northern Colombia, has a particle *ni* which he glosses as "reminder" and which indicates that both speaker and hearer are aware of the proposition (Palmer 1986:76). The Siouan language Hidatsa, according to Matthews (1965:99–100), has what he calls the QUOTATIVE which "indicates that the speaker regards what he has said to be something that everyone knows." Corum (1975:95) describes the Basque particle *ba*, which "coaxes the hearer into accepting or believing the content of the proposition" to which it is joined, as similar to the "sneaky use" of sentential adverbs in English like *obviously, no doubt, surely,* and *needless to say*.

In the case of Norwegian *jo*, there are a variety of ways in which the information may be available to the addressee. Examples of these are given in (72)–(85) below. The information may be available through general cultural knowledge, or it may be available in the discourse or extralinguistic context. Further, it may be information which the addressee might expect but not know to be the case. Prince (1979, 1981) has done much to explore the possible distinctions between types of given information. The point here, however, is not to establish discrete categories of givenness with respect to the information presented in the *jo* proposition, but rather to show a progression from cases where the information is obviously given to those where it is not nearly so obvious. Finally, examples (86)–(93) show where the information is merely a subjective evaluation of the speaker or where it clearly is not given information. The ultimate aim of the entire discussion is to lead us to question whether indeed "proposition as given" is an adequate description of the effect of the particle.

In order to simplify the presentation, word-for-word glossing is omitted in the following examples and throughout chapters four and five. Instead, the original and free translation are given, the particle of interest bracketed by parentheses and included in the free translation in the clause where it occurs.

A Functional Analysis of *jo* and *nå*

Information in context. The following are examples of *jo* propositions whose information is available in the linguistic or situational context.

(72) (G11-2)[1]
Jeg tviler ikke på at det er et sunt liv, men jeg mener: De er jo ikke helt ung lenger, og hvis De så ikke har lagt Dem opp noe...

I don't doubt that it is a healthy life, but I mean: You aren't *(jo)* altogether young any more, and if you haven't saved anything up...

(73) (CA51-1)
(H has just had an encounter with S's father, who came to the door trying to get his daughter back)

H: *Fortell om faren din. Det er ingen skam. Vet du at i sekstiårene så hatet alle foreldrene sine. Det er ikke din skyld.*
S: *Jeg hater dem ikke. De har alltid vært snille mot meg. Jeg har fått alt... de er glade i meg... de passer på meg... alle må ha noen til å passe på seg... ikke sant, Karl...*
H: *(avbryter) Her tror jeg en annen må ta over. For jeg har jo hatt æren av å møte faren din. Og når han kom hit og ville tiltvinge seg en av mannskapet, så var det bare én ting å gjøre.*

H: Tell about your father. It's no shame. Did you know that in the sixties everyone hated their parents? It's not your fault.
S: I don't hate them. They have always been good to me. I have gotten everything... they love me... they take care of me... everyone needs someone to take care of them... right Karl?...

---

[1]The data corpus citation code indicates the source of the example. The following are codes for examples taken from published sources (see the bibliography for full references):
Stigen, 1987: G—Gartneren, A—Angiveren, B—Batteriet, K—Kisten
Christensen, 1986: CA—Columbus ankomst, KED—Kvitt eller dobbelt
Berntzen, 1976: JH—Jan Herwitz
Other data codes indicate unpublished sources, such as personal letters, etc.

H: (interrupting) Here I think someone else will have to take over. Because I have *(jo)* had the honor of meeting your father. And when he came here and wanted to forcefully take with him one of the crew there was only one thing to do.

(74) (G21-1)
G: *Her er nellikene Deres.*
D: *Men der er jo bare syv, jeg skulle ha ti. Det var Gudrun som skulle ha syv roser.*

G: Here are your carnations.
D: But there are *(jo)* only seven, I wanted ten. It was Gudrun who asked for seven roses.

(75) (KED61-1)
F: *I morgen skal vi ut og hente inn eplene. Fire fullpakkete trær. Ett til hver av oss!*
U: *Jeg kan ikke bli med.*
F: *Kan ikke bli med?! Vi drar jo ut alle sammen hvert år. Det vet du da.*

F: Tomorrow we're going to go pick the apples. Four cram-packed trees. One for each of us.
U: I can't go.
F: Can't go?! We all go *(jo)* out every year. You know that.

(76) (CA13-2)
A: *Hva var det du sa om de rakettene? ... Jeg håper ingen ble skadet.*
B: *Det er en feil ved deg, Karl, en brist i din personlighet. Du skal alltid bekymre deg.*
A: *Det er jeg som skal bo her. Det er mine naboer. Meningen var jo at det skulle være en rolig aften. Bursdag og innvielse. Var det ikke?*

A: What was that you said about those rockets? ... I hope nobody got injured.
B: There's one problem with you, Karl, a fault in your personality: you always have to worry.

A: It's ME that has to live here. They are MY neighbors. The idea was *(jo)* that it would be a quiet evening. Us four. Birthday and housewarming party, wasn't it?

(77) (G10-2)
Men for å komme til saken—ja, det er jo De som er gartner Flohris—?

But to get down to business—er, you ARE *(jo)* gardener Flohris—?

General knowledge. In the following examples the information in the *jo* prepositions is available through general cultural knowledge.

(78) (GF2-4)
Jeg blir på en måte litt flau over å bare være så opptatt av "de nære ting" for tida, men jeg synes det er skjønt å stå med begge beina oppi det—det er jo bare en gang i livet!

(talking about making wedding plans) I get a little embarrassed in a way about being so caught up in everyday things these days, but I think it's nice to be totally involved in it—it's *(jo)* only once in a lifetime!

(79) (GF3-1)
Gledelig å høre at dere har fått tilbud om hus—internatliv har jo sine fordeler, men jammen kan det være slitsomt i lengda.

Good to hear that you have been offered a house—dorm life has *(jo)* its advantages, but boy can it be tiresome after awhile.

(80) (CA16-1)
A: *Skal vi ta oppvasken, Kirsten?*
B: *Noen må jo gjøre det.*

A: Shall we do the dishes, Kirsten?
B: Someone has to *(jo)* do it.

Expected information. The information in the *jo* clause may not necessarily be known to the addressee, but may in some cases merely be something that the speaker feels the addressee may expect to be the case.

(81) (CA47-1)
(The speaker is telling a story about a boy who was caught shoplifting by the store-owner.)

*Drittsekken av en eier hadde sagt han ikke skulle melde fra til purken, men derimot skulle han **kanskje** si fra til skolen og foreldrene. **Kanskje**. Og fra den dagen forandra fyren seg. Turde jo ikke si det selv, og gikk og venta på katastrofen støtt.*

The creep of an owner had said he wouldn't report him to the cops, but instead he MIGHT tell the school and his parents. MIGHT. And from that day the guy changed. He didn't (*jo*) dare to tell them himself, just went around constantly waiting for the catastrophe.

(82) (G9-1)
Gartneren, Nils Joachim Flohris, var en av de første som kom hit til dette stedet. Han var en liten forsagt mann med brune hender. Alt som barn hadde han en skrekk for å trå på blomster, han gikk med små utsøkte trinn og virket egentlig litt komisk. Når det var stille omkring ham—og det var det jo som oftest i den første tid—snakket han med blomstene på et språk som bare han og de forsto.

The gardener, Nils Joachim Flohris, was one of the first who came to this place. He was a small, mousy man with brown hands. Even as a child he had a fear of stepping on flowers, he walked with tiny, delicate steps and actually looked a little comical. When it was quiet around him—and it was (*jo*) usually quiet in the beginning—he talked to the flowers in a language that only he and they understood.

Here the information in the *jo* clause might be expected in light of the information presented earlier, namely that the gardener was one of the first to come to this place.

(83) (RT6-1)
(In this example it is the occurrence of *jo* in the last clause which illustrates this type.)

Hilde har hatt lungebetennelse og var verkeleg dårleg. Onsdag for halvannen veke sidan var det avslutning hjå oss for Målfrid sine speleelevar. Den dagen hadde Hilde over 40 i feber. Dr.

A Functional Analysis of *jo* and *nå*

Lind har jo ei dotter som spelar, så både han og kona kom. Då spelingi var over, sa han at dersom me ville skulle han reisa heim etter sakene sine og sjå på Hilde. Me var jo berre glad for det.

Hilde has had pneumonia and was really sick. Wednesday, a week-and-a-half ago, was the recital for Målfrid's piano pupils. That day Hilde had a fever of over 104. Dr. Lind has a daughter who takes lessons, so both he and his wife were here. When the recital was over, he said that if we wanted he would go home and get his things and take a look at Hilde. We were (*jo*) glad for that.

(84) (GF1-6)
Å gå gravid forandrer virkelig fokus og framtidsplaner så det er en merkelig følelse å nå være "fri" igjen. Vi var jo bare kjempeglad for å skulle bli foreldre, men nå kan jeg tillate meg å forstørre opp de ulempene det ville medføre...

Being pregnant really changes one's focus and future plans, so it's a strange feeling to be "free" again. We were (*jo*) overjoyed that we were about to be parents, but now I can allow myself to see all the disadvantages it would entail...

(85) (A33-2)
(V is telling M about another man. V knew him when he was a boy in school, but M did not.)

Han var redd. Turde ikke stå midt utpå skolegården. Og borte ved jentedoen var han noenlunde trygg, for der var bestandig piker fra syvende klassen. De beskyttet ham på et vis. De begynte jo å bli voksne, med bryster og greier, små mødre. Og selv de verste råtassene hadde en slags respekt for dem.

He was afraid. Didn't dare to stand out in the middle of the playground. And over by the girls' restroom he was somewhat safe, because there were always girls there from the seventh grade. They protected him in a way. They were starting (*jo*) to be grown up, with breasts and stuff, little mothers. And even the worst scoundrels had a kind of respect for them.

Subjective evaluation. In many cases, the *jo* clause constitutes a subjective evaluation of some state of affairs by the speaker. In this case the addressee could not be expected to already have access to the information presented.

(86) (CA29-1)
(B is afraid her parents are worrying about where she is, and is in a hurry to contact them.)

A: *Fikk du ringt hjem?*
B: *(bekymret) Det var ingen som svarte.*
A: *(lettet) Da er det jo ingenting som haster.*

A: Were you able to call home?
B: (worried) No one answered.
A: (relieved) Then there's *(jo)* no hurry.

(87) (CA33-1)
A: *Jeg trodde vi skulle ha det... litt hyggelig.*
B: *Hyggelig? Ja, nå skal vi ha det hyggelig. Har vi det hyggelig?*
A: *Du er motbydelig.*
B: *(ler) Dere skjønner jo ikke spøk.*

A: I thought we were going to have... a nice time.
B: A nice time? Okay, now we're going to have a nice time. Are we having a nice time?
A: You're repulsive.
B: (laughs) You guys can't *(jo)* take a joke.

(88) (IB7-2)
Vi er i en tid da alt kan skje angående bosted/jobb/familie. Og det er jo ganske spennende (og litt skummelt) å skulle flytte sammen!

We are in a time when anything can happen as far as apartment/job/family. And it is *(jo)* pretty exciting (and a little scary) to be moving together!

A Functional Analysis of *jo* and *nå* 57

(89) (AGD9-4)
... *det er godt vi ikke vet alle detaljer om hva som skal skje. Det eneste vi vet er at Gud tar omsorg for oss—og leder oss—og mere behøver vi jo ikke vite.*

... it's a good thing we don't know all the details of what's going to happen. The only thing we know is that God will take care of us—and lead us—and more than that we don't need to *(jo)* know.

(90) (A42-1)
(V is trying to talk M into having some sympathy for the traitor and letting him go.)

V: *Det er sinnsvakt.*
M: *Enig med deg.*
V: *Jeg mener: vi står her og vet at det kunne vært en av oss.*
M: *Du kanskje. Ikke jeg.*
V: *Men da er det jo meningsløst. Bare blanke, idiotiske ...*
M: *... tilfeldigheten. Som når et tog går av sporet. Javel. Men nettopp derfor kan du gjøre det. Tenk på den friheten du har.*

V: It's crazy.
M: You're right.
V: I mean: we stand here knowing that it could have been one of us.
M: You maybe, not me.
V: But then it's *(jo)* meaningless. Just pure idiotic...
M: ... matter of chance. Like when a train derails. Okay. But that's why you can do it. Think about the freedom you have.

Information not available to addressee. It is conceivable that the speaker might treat a subjective evaluation as old information. In his thinking it may be so obvious that it hardly counts as an addition to the pragmatic universe of discourse. Likewise, information that the speaker regards as expected or predictable to both speaker and addressee could conceivably be treated as old information. However, there are cases in which the *jo* clause contains a proposition which does not meet any of the above criteria, i.e., where the information does seem to be entirely new.

(91) (CA40-1)
A: *(forsiktig) Du ... er du ... gravid?*
B: *Hvordan vet du det?*
A: *Stakkar ...*
B: *(ler) Du behøver ikke trøste meg. Jeg er ikke syk. Jeg er glad. Jeg er glad for at jeg skal ha barn.*
A: *Vet han det?*
B: *Nei, ikke ennå.* (pause) *Det er jo ikke helt sikkert.*

A: (cautiously) Hey ... ? Are you ... pregnant?
B: How did you know?
A: Poor thing ...
B: (laughs) You don't need to comfort me. I'm not sick. I'm glad. I'm glad that I'm going to have a baby.
A: Does he know?
B: No, not yet. (pause) I'm *(jo)* not really sure yet.

(92) (KED 63-1)
F: *Hvorfor spiser du ikke?*
U: *Herman er på slankekur.*
F: *Du skal spise opp maten.*
H: *Jeg er jo mett!*

F: Why aren't you eating?
U: Herman is on a diet.
F: You're gonna finish your food.
H: I'm *(jo)* full!

(93) (A37-1)
(V is telling a friend about a boy he knew in school, whom the listener knows nothing about.)

V: *Jeg sa at vi var ikke venner, han og jeg. Og det var vi heller ikke. Men efter den dagen da jeg fulgte ham hjem, var det akkurat som jeg følte meg medskyldig i alt som hendte ham. Forklar det hvordan du vil, jeg bare følte det sånn. Det var da jeg begynte å hviske til ham i timen.*
M: *Hviske?*
V: *Ja, når han ble hørt. Han kunne jo aldri noe. Ikke at han var dum, men det som gikk inn i hodet hans kom ikke ut igjen.*

A Functional Analysis of *jo* and *nå*

V: I said that we weren't friends, he and I. And we weren't either. But after the day I went home with him, it was just as if I felt partly guilty for everything that happened to him. Explain it however you want, I just felt that way. It was then I started whispering to him in class.
M: Whispering?
V: Yeah, when the teacher quizzed him. He never knew *(jo)* anything. Not that he was dumb, but what went in to his head didn't come out again.

Speaker strategy. Not only may the *jo* clause sometimes carry information not actually available to the addressee, but conversely, propositionalizing given information is not sufficient criteria for using the *jo* particle.

Suppose a husband comes in the door of his home and upon seeing his wife for the first time since that morning says:

(94) *Å, du har vært hos frisøren idag.*

Oh, you've been to the hairdresser today.

He is stating given information, available to both speaker and hearer. The force of his utterance is best described as a comment. The speaker is indicating his awareness of something in the immediate environment which, in this case, is already known to the addressee. Yet in this context, were the *jo* particle to be used, it would carry implications of some other purpose for the utterance than merely an offhand comment on something available to speaker and addressee.

Imagine now a slightly different context. The husband and wife are sitting at the dinner table discussing the events of their day.

(95) Wife: *Jeg har vært så ueffektiv idag. Har ikke fått sendt ut et eneste julekort.*
Husband: *Du har jo vært hos frisøren.*

Wife: I have been so unproductive today. Haven't gotten a single Christmas card sent out.
Husband: You have *(jo)* been to the hairdresser.

Here the force of the husband's utterance is more than just to make a comment. His utterance has a force beyond the conveyance of information or merely commenting on obvious facts. We might say he has a distinct purpose or strategy for his utterance, and for using the *jo* particle. This strategy translates into an implicature conveyed by the utterance beyond merely the literal meaning of the proposition, something along the lines of:

(96)　You've been to the hairdresser's (and THAT ought to count for SOMETHING).

This might be conveyed in English by prosodic features, such as extra stress on 'hairdresser's', plus an intonation pattern ending in a nonfinal mid-tone.

Consider another situation, this time in a classroom. The teacher is quizzing Geir on his history lesson.

(97)　T: *Nå skal jeg høre om dere har lest til timen idag. Geir, hvem var Hannibal?*
　　　G: *Han var en karthaginsk general.*
　　　T: *Hva er han kjent for?*
　　　G: *Han angrep Roma.*
　　　T: *Riktig!*

　　　T: All right, now I will find out if you've all read your lesson for today. Geir, who was Hannibal?
　　　G: He was a Carthaginian general.
　　　T: What is he known for?
　　　G: He attacked Rome.
　　　T: Correct!

In the above example, although the information contained in both of Geir's utterances is known to the addressee, use of the *jo* particle is not possible. In both utterances, the purpose of the speaker in conveying given information is merely to comply with the request of the teacher. These are what have been called QUIZ-QUESTIONS, to distinguish them from TRUE QUESTIONS, whose purpose is actually to seek information, or RHETORICAL QUESTIONS, whose purpose is not to be answered at all, but merely to make a point.

However, if we change the context slightly and suppose that the teacher, instead of questioning for the purpose of finding out if Geir has done his reading, is actually trying to discern Geir's personal analysis of the lesson, we might get replies from Geir with the same propositional content, but where the *jo* particle would be very appropriate.

(98)　T: *Nå vil jeg tenke litt på hva som måtte drevet denne mannen Hannibal. Geir, hvorfor tror du han hatet Romerne?*

A Functional Analysis of *jo* and *nå* 61

> G: *Han var jo en kartaginsk general.*
> T: *Og hvorfor ville Romerne hatet ham?*
> G: *Han angrep jo Roma.*
>
> T: Now I'd like to think for just a bit about what forces drove this man Hannibal. Geir, why do you suppose Hannibal hated the Romans?
> G: He was *(jo)* a Carthaginian general.
> T: And why should the Romans have hated him?
> G: He attacked *(jo)* Rome.

In this second example, Geir is no longer merely providing information. Each of his utterances has a greater significance than mere information-bearers, that is, they convey an implicature beyond the literal meaning of the proposition. The given information in his utterances is offered as an argument for the conclusions he is drawing. The statement of the facts is only a part of it—he is making a judgment as to the relevance of these facts to the teacher's questions, or more broadly, to the communication situation. And he is hoping the teacher will agree with him. So then, the *jo* proposition is offered as a base, upon which recourse is made for the purpose of accomplishing a larger interactional goal.

The point here is that the speaker has some strategic purpose for encoding the utterance as already known and accepted by the addressee. In the case where the *jo* proposition includes information which is actually not already known to the addressee, we must assume that the speaker has some strategic reason for wishing to give the impression that the proposition is known. What these possible strategies or interactional goals might be is the topic of §§4.1.3 through 4.1.6.

4.1.3 Supportive *jo*

Perhaps the most frequent occurrences of *jo* are in clauses which in some way support a prior utterance by the same speaker. These are typically used in arguments to advance the position of the speaker by giving support to his assertions.

Supportive of an assertion. This is perhaps the most common structure using the *jo* particle. Viewed in a speech-act framework, the clause with *jo* is strengthening some felicity condition of the clause which it supports. The sense of the *jo* clause may usually be captured in English by an utterance prefaced with 'After all...', although there are structures in which this would not sound completely natural in English.

(99) (GF2-2)
Liker ikke at kjolen skal være så viktig, det viktigste er jo å trives på dagen.

I don't like the idea that the wedding dress becomes so important; after all, the most important thing is *(jo)* to enjoy the day.

Here the *jo* clause gives a reason for the previous assertion. Making use of Searle's types of felicity conditions, we might say that the *jo* clause strengthens a preparatory condition, one preparatory condition being the requirement that the speaker (S) has evidence for the truth of the proposition (p). Note, that in terms of Searle's classificatory scheme (1969:66), the *jo* clause itself is not an assertion, or at best is a hedged one, in that another preparatory condition, namely that "it is not obvious to both S and H [addressee] that H knows (does not need to be reminded of, etc.) p" is being hedged.

(100) (G14-1)
Det eneste dere kan gjøre er å forhandle med ham, få ham til å selge godvillig. Det kan vel ikke være så vrient. Det er jo bare et spørsmål om pris. Alle ting har sin pris, sier du.

The only thing you can do is to deal with him, get him to sell voluntarily. That can't be so difficult. It's *(jo)* only a question of price. Everything has its price, you said.

(101) (G9-2)
A: *Kanskje er det blitt mote igjen å tro på denslags siden De dyrker den planten.*
B: *Å—De mener—nei, jeg selger dem ikke. De er jo ikke akkurat noen prydplanter.*

A: Maybe it's become fashionable again to believe in that sort of thing since you're growing that plant.
B: Oh—you mean—no, I don't sell them. They're *(jo)* not exactly a decorative plant.

A Functional Analysis of *jo* and *nå* 63

(102) (K96-1)
(on his knees trying to look through the keyhole of an old chest)

Rart jeg ikke skal få øye på noen ting. Nøkkelhullet er jo så stort som en tommeltott.

Strange that I can't see anything. The keyhole is *(jo)* as big as a thumb.

(103) (G21-2)
A: *Grønt passer i hvert fall ikke til de rosene.*
B: *Visst gjør det det. Det var jo det samme jeg fikk sist.*

A: Well I can tell you for sure that GREEN doesn't match those roses.
B: Sure it does. It was *(jo)* the same color I got last time.

(104) (G14-2)
Herregud, det må da finnes en eller annen måte å få vridd dette på. Vi kan jo ikke stoppe opp på grunn av ... en erindring. Da ville jo alt stoppe.

Good Lord, there must be some way to work this out. We can't *(jo)* stop because of ... a memory. Then everything would *(jo)* come to a halt.

(105) (RT115)
Halvard fekk seg ein kraftig diare så fredag morgon klarte han ikkje stå opp. Tormod vart helt fortvila. Han har jo fylgd morfaren i arbeid kvar dag.

Halvard came down with terrible diarrhea so Friday morning he couldn't get out of bed. Tormod was so upset. He has *(jo)* gone to work with his grandpa every day.

(106) (RT123)
De har vel kanskje høyrt om algeinvasjonen på Sørlandet og opp til Karmøydistriktet? Plutseleg var dei vekk. Takk og lov! Dei drap jo alt som kom i deira veg.

You've probably heard about the algae invasion in the south and up to the Karmøy district? Suddenly they were gone. Thank goodness! They killed *(jo)* everything in their path.

Supportive of a request. The *jo* clause may serve to support a speech act with the force of a request.

(107) (G16-1)
Kunne De ikke grave et annet sted—her er jo så god plass overalt?

Couldn't you dig somewhere else—there's *(jo)* plenty of room all over.

Supportive of a command. The utterance with *jo* may give grounds for a command.

(108) (A33-1)
V: *(nervøst) Må vi vente til det toget kommer?*
M: *Ja, vi må det. Blir bare bråk ellers—hvis naboene skulle høre noe.*
V: *Hvis han skulle skrike, mener du?*
M: *Ja. For eksempel. Et eller annet. Se her, tenn deg en sigarett og ta det med ro. Du behøver jo ikke foreta deg noe—hvis du ikke vil. Men du ba sjæl om å få bli med.*

V: (nervously) Do we have to wait until the train comes?
M: Yes, we have to. Just be trouble otherwise—if the neighbors should hear anything.
V: If he should scream, you mean?
M: Yeah. For example. Something or other. Look here, have a cigarette and take it easy. YOU don't *(jo)* need to do anything—if you don't want to. But it was you who asked to come along.

Supportive of a question. The *jo* proposition may be used to justify a question.

(109) (A39-1)
(The traitor has discovered that he is being watched.)

Jeg visste det også. Hele tiden. Hvor er sigarettene? Her! Én igjen. Men jeg har ingen fyrstikker. Hvorfor kjøpte jeg ikke fyrstikker imorges! Hvorfor har ingen gitt meg beskjed—de hadde jo lovet å si fra hvis noe skulle—de er pliktige til å beskytte meg.

And I knew it too. All along. Where are my cigarettes? Here! One left. But I don't have any matches. Why didn't I buy matches this morning! Why hasn't anyone told me—they promised *(jo)* to let me know if something should—they are obligated to protect me.

(110) (G26-3)
    A: *(De skal) kjøre ned gjerdet. Og begynne planeringen.*
    B: *Men blomstene da? Det står jo ennå mange. Jeg lurer på om jeg kunne ta med noen tel kona?*

    A: (You are to) bulldoze the fence down. And start leveling the ground.
    B: But what about the flowers? There are *(jo)* still a lot of them all over. I wonder if I could take a few home to my wife?

(111) (G24-1)
    Hvor er lysbryteren? Den skal jo være her—ved døren.

    Where is the light switch? It's *(jo)* supposed to be here—by the door.

Supportive of total speech act. Note, from the above example, that the *jo* clause supports not the literal meaning of the preceding proposition, but the illocutionary force of the utterance. The following example illustrates this more clearly. In (111), although the supported proposition is a question, it has the force of a rejection of H's prior suggestion. Thus the *jo* clause supports the previous utterance as a rejection, giving reasons for rejecting, rather than giving reasons for asking a question as also shown in (112).

(112) (G25-1)
    A: *Jaggu knuser'n ikke drivhuset.*
    B: *Vi må si fra til noen.*
    A: *Hvem skal vi si fra til? Det er jo hanses blomster.*

    A: God, he's smashing the greenhouse.
    B: We've got to tell someone.
    A: Who are we going to tell? They are *(jo)* his flowers.

Further examples show that the domain of the supportive relationship may exceed even the illocutionary force of the preceding utterance, and extend to the implicatures which this utterance conveys. This suggests that the supportive *jo* should be understood as supporting a previous speech act in its entire conversational function. Consider the following examples.

(113) (HMH12)
Bare noen dager etter jeg var kommet fra England, fikk jeg brev fra W-kontoret i Oslo. Det var Øyvind Ø. som skriver. Jeg visste ikke at det var han som hadde overtatt etter deg, Erik. Jeg kjenner jo Wenche, konen.

Just a few days after I came back from England, I got a letter from the W-office in Oslo. It was from Øyvind Ø. I didn't know that he was the one who took over after you, Erik. I know *(jo)* Wenche, his wife.

Here the *jo* utterance supports a previous utterance 'I didn't know that he was the one who took over after you, Erik,' which implies 'I am especially interested in this'. The *jo* utterance supports this implication, giving the reasons for the speaker's special interest.

(114) (G10–2)
(The speaker arrives at the house intending to talk to the gardener. He meets a man outside in the garden, and they talk for a while.)

Men for å komme til saken—ja, det er jo De som er gartner Flohris—?

But to get down to business—er, I take it you are *(jo)* gardener Flohris—?

Here the speaker, in the first part of the utterance, implies that he has come because he has some business to discuss, and intends to discuss it with the addressee. The *jo* utterance indicates his rationale for doing so, that is, because the addressee is in fact the person whom he intended to speak to.

4.1.4 Oppositional *jo*

The usage of *jo*, to which we turn our attention now, expresses opposition to an idea or implication presented in a previous utterance by the

A Functional Analysis of *jo* and *nå* 67

addressee. Here the speaker makes recourse to an implied or assumed consensus in order to give force to his opposition. The speaker is reminding the addressee of some proposition which he feels the addressee ought to have been aware of, and which, had he been aware of, would have kept him from conveying the implication which is being opposed. Thus the speaker is communicating his censure of the addressee for needing the reminder. The utterance may convey impatience with the addressee.

(115) (CA34-1)
   A: *Jeg er av den oppfatning at vi må befri Karl for hans dårlige samvittighet.*
   B: *(irritert) Hva er det du snakker om, "dårlig samvittighet?"*
   A: *Dere ser det vel. Gutten er i konstant bakrus.*
   C: *Det tror jeg virkelig ikke han er alene om i dag.*
   A: *Men Karl er alltid i bakrus. Karl er alltid plaget.*
   B: *Plaget av hva?*
   A: *Dårlig samvittighet, sa jeg jo.*

   A: I am of the opinion that we must free Karl of his guilty conscience.
   B: (irritated) What are you talking about, "guilty conscience?"
   A: You can see it, can't you? The boy suffers from a perennial hangover.
   C: I really don't think he's alone in that today.
   A: But Karl ALWAYS has a hangover. Karl is always suffering.
   B: Suffering from what?
   A: Guilty conscience, I said *(jo)*.

(116) (CA14-1)
   A: *Hvorfor har du ikke tatt på deg buksene?*
   B: *Jeg sa jo at de er borte!*

   A: Why haven't you put on your pants?
   B: I said *(jo)* that they're gone!

In the following example Karl had said earlier that he thought the bell had rung, but then concluded that he must have dreamt it.

(117) (CA37-2)
    A: *Der kom jeg på noe. Faren din har vært her.*
    B: *(forskrekket) Har faren til Synnøve vært her?*
    A: *Akkurat. Når var det? Jentene var ute og du sov.*
    C: *(nesten på gråten) Hvorfor har du ikke sagt det før?*
    A: *Hadde helt glemt det.*
    B: *Det var det jeg sa. At det ringte på.*
    A: *Du drømte jo bare det.*

    A: I just remembered something. Your father has been here.
    B: (horrified) Has Synnøve's father been here?
    A: Right. When was it now? The girls were out and you were sleeping.
    C: (almost crying) Why haven't you said so earlier?
    A: Completely forgot.
    B: That's what I said. That the doorbell rang.
    A: You just dreamt *(jo)* that.

The oppositional *jo* may have the force of a protest.

(118) (KED61-2)
(Mother to son at dinner table)

Du spiser jo ingenting, Herman!

You're not eating *(jo)* anything, Herman!

(119) (CA24-1)
    H: *Hvorfor kan vi ikke snakke om det . . . om alt!*
    K: *Du fleiper jo bare!*

    H: Why can't we talk about it . . . about everything!
    K: You just joke *(jo)* around!

(120) (G11-1)
    A: *De kunne ikke tenke Dem å selge oss noe av grunnen her?*
    B: *Av haven? Selge?*
    A: *Ja. Fire-fem mål for eksempel.*
    B: *Men det er jo halvparten!*

A: You wouldn't consider selling us part of your property here, would you?
B: Of the garden? Sell?
A: Yes. Four or five acres for example.
B: But that's *(jo)* half!

(121) (CA38-1)
S: *Har faren min vært her!? Var han ikke sint?*
H: *Slett ikke. Han spurte etter deg og ble selvfølgelig rørt over at du var ute og ringte hjem.*
K: *Du kunne godt sagt dette litt før, Hans.*
H: *Men alt er jo i sin skjønneste orden. Vi ble verdens beste venner.*

S: Has my father been here!? Wasn't he mad?
H: Not at all. He asked for you and was naturally touched that you were out calling home.
K: You sure could have told us before, Hans.
H: But everything is *(jo)* just fine. We became best of friends.

4.1.5 Concessive *jo*

Another frequent usage of *jo* is to mark a proposition that hedges or retracts a previous utterance of the speaker or the implications thereof (cf. Brown and Levinson 1978:166 for a discussion on the Tzeltal particle *taan*.) Often a natural English translation of this type is possible with the pragmatic device, 'of course...' or contrastive stress on the verb:

(122) (G18-1)
A: *Har ikke dere også en sånn lov som sier hva som er riktig, som forteller hva dere skal gjøre?*
B: *Lov—tja. William, har vi noen lov som sier oss hva vi skal gjøre?*
C: *Nei sannelig om jeg vet—vi har jo diverse lover, de fleste av dem er bare i veien.*

A: Don't you people also have the kind of law that says what's right, that tells you what you should do?
B: Well...law...hmm...William, do we have any law that tells us what to do?

C: Well, heck if I know... we have *(jo)* various laws, most of them are just in the way.

The *jo* particle may occur with an utterance initial *men* 'but', which is a pragmatic marker indicating that the present utterance in some way contrasts with something in the preceding discourse. The resultant effect is to signal that the speaker is retreating from the conclusions or implications of his prior utterance. In (123)–(124) the pragmatic *men* occurs in the same clause as *jo*:

(123) (AGD7-1)
Jeg har valgt å være i Oslo hele sommeren. Ta imot gjennomreisende besøk—og utforske sommer-Oslo. Skal ha de 2 siste ferieukene i månedskiftet aug-sept. Jeg er glad for valget men det medfører jo en liten belastning på jobb i.o.m. at det skiftes ut med ferievikarer hele tiden både leger og pleiere. Det er litt slitsomt.

I've decided to stay in Oslo all summer. Receive visitors travelling through town and explore Oslo in the summer. I'll take my vacation the last two available weeks around the end of August, beginning of September. I'm glad for my decision, but it does *(jo)* involve a little extra effort at work, in that the whole time there will be a lot of vacation substitutes for both doctors and nurses. That's a little tiring.

(124) (CA37-1)
Himmelen er usynlig. Ingen andre fartøy er i sikte. Men det må jo være flere. Vi var mange da vi dro ut.

The sky is invisible. There are no other vessels in sight. But there must *(jo)* be more. There were many of us when we set sail.

(125) (G21-3)
A: *Så du hendene hans? Et øyeblikk var jeg virkelig redd.*
B: *Bo sånn alene, vet du. Ikke engang en husholderske.*
A: *Denne Miriam han snakket om?*
B: *Det var visst konen hans. Men hun døde jo for mange år siden.*

A Functional Analysis of *jo* and *nå* 71

A: Did you see his hands? For a moment there I was really afraid.
B: Lives alone, you know. Not even a housekeeper.
A: This Miriam he was talking about?
B: That was apparently his wife. But she died *(jo)* many years ago.

(126) (AGD7-4)
Er spent på hvordan de blir som foreldre. Kan ikke helt forestille meg dem i den rollen. Men—rollene endres jo stadig.

I'm excited to see how they'll be as parents. Can't really picture them in that role. But—roles change *(jo)* all the time.

The next set of examples is slightly different, in that the pragmatic *men* occurs in the clause FOLLOWING the *jo* clause. The result is that the speaker signals a retreat from a prior utterance or its implications, and then having done this hedging, subsequently returns to supporting it.

(127) (GF3-1)
Gledelig å høre at dere har fått tilbud om hus—internatliv har jo sine fordeler, men jammen kan det være slitsomt i lengda.

Nice to hear that you've been offered a house—dorm life has *(jo)* its advantages, but it sure can be tiresome in the long run.

(128) (GF1-6)
Å gå gravid forandrer virkelig fokus og framtidsplaner så det er en merkelig følelse å nå være fri igjen. Vi var jo bare kjempeglad for å skulle bli foreldre, men nå kan jeg tillate meg å forstørre opp de ulempene det ville medføre...

Being pregnant really changes one's focus and future plans, so it's a strange feeling to be free again. We were *(jo)* overjoyed that we were about to be parents, but now I can allow myself to see all the disadvantages it would entail.

Occasionally the speaker will be hedging an utterance further back in the exchange which is separated from the *jo* clause by an intervening turn of the addressee. In this case the speaker is signalling his agreement with the addressee's intervening turn, at the same time hedging or retracting his earlier opinion. (Note that in the following examples, it is the particle NOT in parentheses in the original which is the example for this case.)

(129) (G21-4)
A: Så du hendene hans? Et øyeblikk var jeg virkelig redd.
B: Bo sånn alene, vet du. Ikke engang en husholderske.
A: Denne Miriam han snakket om?
B: Det var visst konen hans. Men hun døde (jo) for mange år siden.
A: Ja det er jo sant. Men allikevel.

A: Did you see his hands? For a moment there I was really afraid.
B: Live alone like that, you know. Not even a housekeeper.
A: This Miriam he was talking about?
B: That was apparently his wife. But she died many years ago.
A: Yes, that's (jo) true. But still.

(130) (G26-2)
A: De kan begynne med å ta vekk gjerdet.
B: Er det ikke litt tidlig, tror du?
A: Nei hvorfor det? Vi har (jo) fått tilsagn fra ham at vi kan sette igang, ikke sant? At han er villig til å selge. Bare muntlig riktignok.
B: Jovisst—jo, det har vi jo—forsåvidt.

A: You can start by taking away the fence.
B: Don't you think it's a little early?
A: No, why should it be? After all, we have his permission to start, right? That he's willing to sell. Just verbally, of course.
B: Oh yeah, yeah sure... I guess we have (jo)... in a way.

4.1.6 Contra-expectational *jo*

In the oppositional *jo*, the idea countered by the particle is present due to some utterance by the addressee. In the concessive, the idea countered was brought about by a previous utterance of the speaker himself. In this next type of *jo* structure, it appears that the idea being countered is not brought about by any utterance of either speaker or addressee, but is an

A Functional Analysis of *jo* and *nå*

assumption or idea present in the mind of the speaker, or which the speaker assumes to be present in the mind of the addressee, due to other contextual factors.

By countering some idea which he has held up until the point of utterance of the *jo* proposition, the speaker may indicate surprise. The addressee of the following utterance has just finished telling what he claimed was an anonymous story about two men visiting the Vatican, when it suddenly occurs to the speaker that the story was about him.

(131) (CA48-1)
(funderer, brått) Det var jo vi! (Tar seg i det stille) Det var jo vi som var i Peterskirken.

(pondering, suddenly) That was *(jo)* us! (catches himself quietly) That was *(jo)* us who were in St. Peter's Basilica.

In the next example, the speaker has just discovered that he is locked inside his post at the missile-battery.

(132) (B68-1)
(rusker i døren) Men i allverden, døren er jo stengt! Hva skal det bety?

(shaking the door) What in the world, the door is *(jo)* locked! What is that supposed to mean?

Note that the first of the above two examples might conceivably be viewed as an oppositional *jo*, in that the idea being countered by the partical utterance was indirectly given rise to by an utterance of the addressee. The second example is clearly contra-expectational, however, in that the idea has no such source. The speaker merely expects the door to be unlocked, having no reason to suppose that he is to be a prisoner at his own post.

In the next example, an old man is just entering the room where a number of other people are sitting. Although he expects the others to be in the room, he is unable to see them, because he has lost his glasses. After groping until he finds his glasses, he puts them on, sees the people, and utters the following:

(133) *Sånn ja. Det var bedre. Her sitter dere jo. Lys levende.*

There we go. That's better. Here you are *(jo)*. Big as life.

Although the old man thought the others might be there, he was unable to see them, and so a doubt arose as to whether they in fact were present. In this case the idea being countered by the *jo* utterance is the doubt in the mind of the old man as to whether he would find the other people.

In other instances, the speaker may counter an idea or expectation which he feels is present in the consciousness of the addressee. In the following example, several people are playing a game where they spin a bottle, then the one to whom the bottle points when it stops must tell a story. At one point in the game when the participants have just finished discussing the last story told, but before the bottle has been spun again, a speaker utters the following and begins to tell a story out of turn.

(134) (CA44-1)
Jeg kan jo legge til en liten historie. Selv om det ikke er min tur.

I can *(jo)* add a story here, even though it's not my turn.

Because the speaker was not expected to tell a story unless he had been chosen by spinning the bottle, he uses the particle to signal that he is going against the addressee's expectations. The effect here is as if the speaker were granting a favor or conceding to tell a story although he was not expected to. Here, however, the speaker is countering an assumed idea, rather than an impression he himself has given in something he said.

In the following example, the speaker uses the particle to oppose an idea which his own utterance could only bring out in a very indirect way.

(135) (CA45-1)
En dame kommer hjem til Norge etter å ha vært på pakketur til Kanariøyene. Alt er såre vel, brun, nypult og brisen. Brunfargen forsvinner jo etterhvert, og hun blir edru.

A lady comes home to Norway after having been on a package tour to the Canary Islands. Everything is just great—she's had her romantic adventures, she's tanned, and she's still tipsy. The tan disappears *(jo)* after awhile, and she gets sober.

Although anyone hearing the story might expect that the tan would fade, the speaker feels the need to propositionalize this in order to make sure that the listeners do not derive the wrong idea that things will continue as described in the first two sentences of the story.

A Functional Analysis of *jo* and *nå*

4.1.7 Reanalysis: *jo* as oppositional

To summarize so far, we have examined four main categories of ways in which the *jo* particle may be used:

1. Supportive
2. Oppositional
3. Concessive
4. Contra-expectational

In the last three, we saw that the *jo* particle has the effect of countering some idea in the discourse context. In the oppositional, the idea countered is seen as originating in a previous utterance of the addressee. In the concessive, the idea countered comes from something the speaker himself has just said. With the contra-expectational, the idea countered cannot be directly attributed to any specific utterance by either speaker or addressee. It is an expectation which has naturally occurred as a result of the speech situation in general or other extralinguistic factors.

The discussion of the semantic reduction of *jo* from response particle to modal particle has shown that a basic feature remaining in the modal sense of *jo* is a polarity reversal, the countering of an expectation. The natural question to ask here then, is if a generalization can be made which will allow the first category, the supportive *jo*, to fit into this analysis. That is, is there something fundamentally different about the supportive *jo* from the other three types, or can it also be conceived of as a countering of expectation.

There are several cases of *jo* usage which appear to be transitional or borderline between a supportive and an oppositional kind of structure. In the following example, two businessmen are discussing how to get an old gardener to agree to sell them his land. They've tried gentle persuasion, but the old man is adamant. They are getting more desperate.

(136) (G15-1)
    A: *Hva faen gjør vi nå?*
    B: *Jeg kom til å tenke på noe.—Den maskinen—gravemaskinen.*
    A: *Ja.*
    B: *Hvis det ikke er for sterkt da.*
    A: *Nåh—du er vel ikke av dem som tar for hardt i.*
    B: *Gubben er jo nokså skral, han tåler nok ikke store støyten.*

A: What the hell do we do now?
B: I just thought of something. That machine—the bulldozer.
A: Yeah.
B: That is, if it isn't too drastic.
A: Nah. You're not one to do anything too tough.
B: The old duffer is *(jo)* pretty feeble, he probably wouldn't stand too big of a shock.

Here B begins to make a proposal, but in his second turn partially retracts it, implying that he thinks it may be so tough on the old man that it would hurt him. A, in his final turn, implies that B's idea surely wouldn't be too tough, and that B's doubts are unfounded. He wants to encourage B to go ahead and make his suggestion. Thus B in his final response, by offering as GIVEN the proposition that the old man is rather feeble, is supporting his previous utterance by adding evidence for its validity. If A's final turn were deleted from this exchange, we would still have a well-formed structure in which B merely followed up his expression of a reservation with a statement of his grounds for that reservation.

At the same time, however, B is countering the implication in A's immediately preceding turn that his suggestion is surely NOT too tough. So we see here that the same *jo* utterance serves both a supportive as well as an oppositional function. And this is of course not surprising, when we consider the nature of an argument as an exchange wherein two speakers have as their goal to convince each other of the validity of their points. Each speaker attempts to counter the arguments of the interlocuter, while at the same time giving the best grounds possible for his own arguments.

In summary then, what we have in the above example is a case where an oppositional *jo* structure is transformed into a supportive structure by deletion of the intervening turn of the addressee.

There is another type of oppositional exchange structure which may be transformed into a supportive structure, this time not by deletion of an intervening H-turn, but rather by insertion of an implied assertion of the speaker. These are structures in which the utterance containing the particle has an illocutionary force which is different than the literal force of the proposition. Consider an example which we have looked at earlier.

A Functional Analysis of *jo* and *nå*   77

(137) (G11-1)
       A: *De kunne ikke tenke Dem å selge oss noe av grunnen her?*
       B: *Av haven? Selge?*
       A: *Ja. Fire-fem mål for eksempel.*
       B: *Men det er jo halvparten!*

       A: You wouldn't consider selling us part of your property here, would you?
       B: Of the garden? Sell?
       A: Yes. Four or five acres for example.
       B: But that's *(jo)* half!

While the literal meaning of the *jo* proposition is only an assertion or clarification of the size of ground the speaker is being asked to sell, the illocutionary force of the utterance is clearly a rejection of the proposal. Were this rejection made explicit, it could appear immediately preceding the *jo* utterance, in which case we would have a well-formed supportive structure as follows:

(138) A: *De kunne ikke tenke Dem å selge oss noe av grunnen her?*
       B: *Av haven? Selge?*
       A: *Ja. Fire-fem mål for eksempel.*
       B: *Nei! Jeg vil ikke selge. Det er jo halvparten!*

       A: You wouldn't consider selling us part of your property here, would you?
       B: Of the garden? Sell?
       A: Yes. Four or five acres for example.
       B: No! I will not sell. That's *(jo)* half!

Consider another example.

(139) (KED61-2)
       (family at dinner table)

       Moren: *Du spiser jo ingenting, Herman.*
       Herman: *Jeg er ikke sulten.*
       Moren: *Det sier du alltid. Er det noe i veien? Eller liker du ikke maten?*
       Herman: *(aggressiv) Jeg er bare ikke sulten! Må vel være lov det?!*

Mother: You aren't *(jo)* eating anything, Herman.
Herman: I'm not hungry.
Mother: You always say that. Is something the matter? Or don't you like the food?
Herman: (aggressive) I'm just not hungry! Nothing in the rules against that, is there?!

Although the literal meaning of the mother's first utterance is merely an assertion that Herman is not eating, it has the illocutionary force of a criticism or a rebuke, possibly an entreaty for him to eat. From Herman's defensive response it is clear that he interprets it as such. The important observation to make here is that the literal meaning of the *jo* proposition supports the illocutionary force of the utterance. This might be represented in the following structure.

(140)   Mother: Herman, please get to work on your supper. You're not eating *(jo)* a thing!

In this case the *jo* proposition supports the previous utterance (representing the illocutionary force of the *jo* utterance) by giving reasons for the mother's concern, i.e., reasons for the entreaty being made.

Consider the following oppositional structure.

(141)   (CA13-1)
A: *Jeg vil hjem.*
B: *Kan vi ikke rydde litt først, og så eter vi frokost.*
A: *Jeg er ikke sulten.* (pause) *Jeg må ihvertfall ringe hjem.*
B: *Jeg har jo ikke telefon.*

A: I want to go home.
B: Let's clean up a little first, and then we'll eat breakfast.
A: I'm not hungry. (pause) At least I've got to call home.
B: I don't have *(jo)* a telephone.

Here, by making the literal assertion that he has no telephone, the speaker is implying 'You can't call home (from here)'. The relationship between literal meaning and implication is again supportive, 'You can't call home because I have no telephone'.

So what we have are oppositional structures where the literal meaning of the *jo* proposition counters an idea believed to be held by the addressee. And precisely this countering implied by the *jo* particle is the trigger for an implication beyond the literal meaning of the proposition. The relationship between the literal meaning of the proposition and its implication is a supportive one.

This connection between the supportive structures and the idea of countering of expectation seems logical. Whenever the speaker feels the need to justify or give grounds for an utterance, he does so because of some opposition to what he is saying, whether this opposition is indicated in some way by the addressee, or merely assumed by the speaker.

So we find the idea of polarity reversal or countering of an expectation to be present even in the supportive usage of the *jo* particle.

One way to show this unity between the supportive and the oppositional exchange structures is by utilizing the representational techniques of conversation analysis, borrowing from Levinson's unique reanalysis of indirect speech acts. He shows that a typical request often involves a sequence of four conversational positions, as follows (Levinson: 1983:358).

Position 1: pre-request
Position 2: go ahead
Position 3: request
Position 4: compliance

Example (142) is Merrit's example taken from Levinson (1983:358).

(142) Position 1: A: Hi. Do you have uh size C   [PRE-REQUEST]
        flashlight batteries?
      Position 2: B: Yes sir.   [GO AHEAD]
      Position 3: A: I'll have four, please.   [REQUEST]
      Position 4: B: [turns to get]   [RESPONSE]

The speaker, Levinson claims, rather than launching right into his request, prefers to check the ability or willingness of his interlocuter to grant the request. Ideally, however, the speaker will not even have to make the request itself (position 3), because hopefully the addressee at the prompting of the pre-request, will offer to comply, or, even more preferred, merely comply at once. Thus the normal turn-sequence of four positions may be collapsed to two, composed of positions 1 and 4. In (143), the second turn actually fills a structural position 4. This example is from Sinclair in Levinson 1983:361.

(143) Have you got Embassy Gold please? [POSITION 1]
Yes dear [provides] [POSITION 4]

Now, using the same approach, we might observe that a normal argumentative exchange is composed of various positions within which the speakers exchange their argumentative points. A simple three-turn argumentative exchange might have the following structure.

Position 1: A: ASSERTION
Position 2: B: OBJECTION/COUNTERPOINT
Position 3: A: RESPONSE TO OBJECTION

For example:

(144) (CA36)
Position 1: A: *Jeg måtte slå lens over ripa.*
Position 2: B: *Du pisset ikke ut av vinduet?!*
Position 3: A: *Dassen er tett som en purk, jo.*

Position 1: A: I had to pee over the railing.
Position 2: B: You didn't piss out the window?!
Position 3: A: The can is clogged as heck, (sure I did).

The structure is a unit, in that the various utterances are defined by the positions in which they occur: B's objection in position 2 refers directly back to A's original assertion, while A's response in position 3 refers back to B's point. Having had his original assertion in position 1 rejected, A's purpose in position 3 is twofold, both to counter B's objection in position 2, and in so doing to reaffirm his own original assertion in position 1.

What is interesting about this structure are the constraints on the nature of the utterance in position 3. There are, specifically, two position-3 move-types which would NOT advance A's purposes. Firstly, and most obviously, it would not serve A's purposes to advance a second assertion in the form of a new proposition. B, having rejected the position 1 assertion, may equally well challenge this new assertion, and A will find himself in the same predicament as before, not having gained any ground in his argument.

Secondly, it would not serve A's purposes to merely restate or insist upon his position 1 assertion. B would have no additional reason to accept the restatement than he had to accept the original point. A's position-3 turn must somehow counter B's position-2 objection, while at the same time reinforcing his original position-1 assertion. And this it must do, according to this argument, without introducing a new assertion which in turn may be challenged by B.

The obvious solution for A is to present a GIVEN in the Aristotelian logical sense, a piece of evidence already accepted as true by speaker and addressee, which will undermine the objection in position 2, and in so doing support the assertion in position 1. This is where the *jo* particle comes in. We have seen above that the basic meaning of the *jo* particle, derived from its use as a question-answering particle, is to signal the countering of an idea or expectation. In the semantic reduction analysis we saw that such a contradiction leads to, or calls for, an explanation in terms of some piece of given, or uncontested information. Both of these components of basic meaning are present here.

In the structure being discussed here, the position-3 utterance is presented as such a piece of information which cannot be contested, i.e., is not subject to argument. Also, the *jo* proposition stands in opposition to the previous turn by the speaker. It is the structural configuration, however, from which the *jo* proposition takes on the supportive characteristic.

Now note what happens when the turn in position 2 is deleted.

(145) (CA36)
Position 1: A: *Jeg måtte slå lens over ripa.*
Position 3: A: *Dassen er jo tett som en purk.*

Position 1: A: I had to pee over the railing.
Position 3: A: The can is (*jo*) clogged as heck.

The exchange is still well-formed, and the position 3 turn carries the same significance, both support and opposition. In this case, however, the opposition is directed to an expected or assumed position-2 objection.

Note that the particle must be moved to postverbal, the TRUE modal particle position. As discussed above, the sentence-final position in the case of *jo* conveys a stronger sense of opposition, closer to the original independent-utterance function. The change in the position of the particle slightly de-emphasizes the oppositional nature of the utterance. It does not seem possible for the particle to remain in the sentence-final position in the supportive structure.

A postverbal particle in position 3 will retain its position when the position-2 turn is deleted:

(146) (G15-1)
Position 1: A: *Hvis det ikke er for sterkt da.*
Position 2: B: *Nåh—du er vel ikke av dem som tar for hardt i.*
Position 3: A: *Gubben er jo nokså skral...*

Position 1: A: That is, if it isn't too drastic.
Position 2: B: Nah—you're not one to do anything TOO tough.
Position 3: A: The old duffer IS *(jo)* pretty feeble...

Again, upon deletion of position 2, the position-3 turn retains both its supportive and oppositional characteristics, and a well-formed supportive structure is formed.

(147) (G15-1)
Position 1: A: *Hvis det ikke er for sterkt da.*
Position 3: A: *Gubben er jo nokså skral.*

Position 1: A: That is, if it isn't too drastic.
Position 3: A: The old duffer IS *(jo)* pretty feeble.

Applying this mechanism to earlier examples of the supportive *jo* where no addressee-turn intervened, we can postulate an underlying position-2 turn to which the *jo* proposition is responding.

(148) (G10-4)
Position 1: A: *Men om de nu for eksempel bare hadde fem mål, ville De ikke da også få plass til de forskjellige artene?*
Position 3: A: *De kunne jo rasjonalisere.*

Position 1: A: But if you, for example, only had five acres, wouldn't you still have room for the various types?
Position 3: A: You could *(jo)* economize.

The speaker, in uttering the *jo* proposition, is countering a potential or imagined objection to his original utterance. A structure such as the above might have the following underlying structure.

(149) (G10-4)

    Position 1: A: *Men om de nu for eksempel bare hadde fem mål, ville De ikke da også få plass til de forskjellige artene?*
    Position 2: B: *Hvordan kunne jeg få plass til alle artene på halvparten av plassen?*
    Position 3: A: *De kunne jo rasjonalisere.*

    Position 1: A: But if you, for example, only had five acres, wouldn't you still have room for the various types?
    Position 2: B: How could I have room for all the types on half the space?
    Position 3: A: You could *(jo)* economize.

Another example, (150), would have the structure shown in (151).

(150) (CA40-1)

    B: *Vet han det (at du skal ha barn)?*
    Position 1: A: *Nei, ikke ennå.*
    Position 3: A: *Det er jo ikke helt sikkert.*

    B: Does he know (that you're going to have a baby)?
    Position 1: A: No, not yet.
    Position 3: A: It's *(jo)* not for sure yet.

(151)

    B: *Vet han det (at du skal ha barn)?*
    Position 1: A: *Nei, ikke ennå.*
    Position 2: B: *Det burde han vite.*
    Position 3: A: *Det er jo ikke helt sikkert.*

    B: Does he know (that you're going to have a baby)?
    Position 1: A: No, not yet.
    Position 2: B: He ought to know.
    Position 3: A: It's *(jo)* not for sure yet.

Franck seems to open the door to an analysis such as the above by making similar use of a conversation analysis framework in her discussion of the German modal particle *doch*. She postulates an *erinnerndes doch* or *doch*-as-reminder, which seems to share many of the properties of Norwegian *jo*. It occurs most frequently in what she calls "conversational narrative text," and has the effect of bringing a fact into memory which the speaker assumes that the addressee knows or is able to know, but which is not present to him at the moment. To reconcile the *doch*-as-reminder with the otherwise oppositional character of *doch*, Franck hypothesizes an underlying or "fictive" turn by a conversational partner, against which the *doch*-utterance is directed:

> In order to reconstruct the connection with the Standard-*doch*, one might at best hypothesize a fictive predecessor—as an empty turn—against which the use of *doch* would be directed... It is within the rights and interest of the given speaker, the narrator, to hold the floor until the end of his narration or argumentation, once his narration has begun and its beginning has been accepted. Moreover, if he does not want to lose the interest of the addressee, the speaker must show the credibility of what he is saying at every stage of the narration. Whether or not he is successful at this will be indicated by the addressee through facial expressions, gestures, or minimal-response-utterances. If something unusual is asserted without further explanation, the credibility of the utterance may be impaired, and the addressee may interrupt with an inserted question. The speaker may, however, as a precaution, anticipate and refute the imagined objection. He may seek to preempt interruptions for two reasons:
>
> 1. The inserted question may be a kind of correction; in which case the rule applies which states: "Self-correction is preferred to other correction" (Sacks 1967).
>
> 2. Narrations and longer argumentation are organized according to a superordinate plan, and an interruption could make necessary a reorganizing of such a plan...
>
> The verbally unmanifested turn of the addressee may be more than merely hypothetical; it may for example be executed by means of certain facial expressions or gestures, or through the omission of minimal-response-confirmations on the part of the addressee. (Franck 1980:182, my translation)

The supportive *jo* clause may be viewed in terms of Aristotelian deductive logic as one of the givens, which when accepted must inevitably lead to the "new" conclusion. And support is typically only needed in some kind of argumentative turn, that is, when the one speaker is COUNTERING or REVERSING the polarity of the other's utterances. A supportive utterance must naturally be an indisputable given, otherwise a new argument would have to be resolved over the truth or falsity of the supportive utterance itself, and so on ad infinitum.

A Functional Analysis of *jo* and *nå*

The polarity reversal of *jo* can be seen in this usage. In the supportive *jo*, the speaker is countering an imagined challenge to his statement by backing it up with the given. As evidence for this, a speaker would not use a supportive *jo* clause if the supported assertion was not somehow controversial.

(152) (initiating comment at bus stop)
Det er fint vær idag.
*Det er jo 30 grader.

Nice weather today.
*It's (jo) 86 degrees.

But:

(153) (initiating comment at bus stop)
A: *Det er fint vær idag.*
B: *Fint nei! Det er kalt! Det ligger jo frost på marken!*

A: Nice weather today.
B: Nice! Huh! It's COLD! There's *(jo)* frost on the ground!

Thus the supportive *jo* on closer examination may be shown to contain the element of polarity reversal which was obvious in the oppositional *jo*. Conversely, the oppositional *jo* was shown to function in a supportive role to the indirect illocutionary force of the utterance. The concessive *jo*, however, is the tie-breaker. It conveys only the polarity-reversal element (in this case, reversal of the speaker's own implication or an idea arising or assumed to arise from the speaker's utterance).

4.1.8 Conclusion

The basic function of *jo*, which we find in all its usages, is thus twofold: first to counter or oppose some idea assumed to be 'in the air,' and second to do this by means of recourse to an implied consensus on the facts. Krivonosov (1977) showed that modal particles have no lexical-semantic meaning proper. Rather, according to Bublitz (1978), the particles function as CONVENTIONAL IMPLICATURES, i.e., inferences attached by convention to particular lexical items or expressions. We might restate the conventional implicature of *jo* as follows:

1. There is consensus on the facts.
2. There is an idea in the air which will be countered by this consensus.

We saw above, however, that further implicatures, called CONVERSATIONAL IMPLICATURES, may be derived from the content of the utterance and the context, plus some specific assumptions about the nature of verbal interaction. In the case of *jo*, we saw that one such assumption is that the speaker has a strategic reason for utilizing the particle, that is, an interactional goal. This assumption, together with the particular interactional context and conversational structure, derives the conversational implicatures associated with the various usages of *jo*. With the supportive *jo*, where the context indicates that the speaker is countering an idea which he imagines may occur to the addressee as a result of his utterance, the conversational implicature derived is that the particle utterance in some way supports or gives grounds for the previous utterance. With the concessive *jo*, the fact that the speaker is countering an idea which he himself is responsible for produces the conversational implicature that the speaker is retracting or conceding something. With the oppositional *jo*, where the speaker is countering an immediately preceding utterance of the addressee, the implicature is one of censure or reminder as opposition to the idea represented in the utterance countered. Finally, with the contra-expectational *jo*, where the context does not indicate that a specific utterance is being responded to by the particle, the speaker is perceived as countering an idea inherent in the discourse context or the extralinguistic context, with the resultant implication of surprise.

4.1.9 *Jo* in monologue text

An additional observation will be made here, and its significance to discourse analysis taken up in the final section of the paper. Both dialogue as well as monologue texts have been analyzed in the present study. Of the various types of usages of *jo* found, only the supportive and concessive occur in both dialogue and monologue. The oppositional and contra-expectational usages occur in the present data corpus only in conversational exchanges between two or more speakers.

Some reflection on the nature of these usages will make clear the reason for this. The basic function of the particle, it has been shown, involves the countering or opposition of some idea present in the speech situation, whether in the mind of the speaker or assumed to be present in the mind of the addressee. Only in the case of the supportive and concessive could such an idea arise within the context of a monologue text. In the concessive, the speaker is hedging an idea which he believes he has created by means of a previous utterance. In the supportive, the speaker attempts to preclude some unwanted idea which he suspects the addressee may entertain in response to his utterance.

With the oppositional usage, in contrast, the countered idea arises through the previous utterance of the addressee, while with the contra-expectational, the idea comes about due to contextual factors partially or entirely outside of the text itself. Thus, barring special devices such as answering one's own rhetorical questions, in neither of these usages would monologue text be sufficient as the source of the idea to be countered.

4.2 Nå

4.2.1 Reduction from *nå* as adverb

The modal particle *nå* appears to have derived by a process of semantic and phonological reduction from its near-homophone, the temporal adverb *nå* 'now' which indicates deictic reference to the present moment. This form occurs stressed, postverbally, as in (154).

(154) *Vi kommer nå   inn til Oslo sentralstasjon.*
      we come   now in to Oslo Central^Station
      We are now arriving at Oslo Central Station.

The beginnings of semantic reduction can be seen in cases where *nå* signals not so much a deictic reference to the present moment, but rather reference to the end-point on a continuum leading up to the present moment. The proposition is presented as true at the present moment as opposed to in the past, i.e., as seen from the perspective common to speaker and hearer AT THE PRESENT MOMENT. This usage of *nå* occurs in a variety of syntactic positions.

Sentence-initial stressed:

(155) *Han er gått. Nå kan du   komme ut.*
      he is gone now can you come out
      He's gone. You can come out now.

Post-verbal stressed:

(156) *Jeg er nå en gift mann.*
 I am now a married man
 I am now a married man.

Sentence-final stressed:

(157) *Du kan gå nå.*
 you can go now
 You can go now.

A further semantically reduced form of *nå* might be called the TEMPORAL CONTINGENCY ADVERBIAL. Here the speaker is presenting the utterance as temporally contingent upon past events of which speaker and addressee are aware at the present moment, something to the effect of 'Because of/in light of past events OF WHICH YOU AND I ARE AWARE...' Note that the speaker is not merely making recourse to the past events themselves, but also to the addressee's awareness of the events.

Sentence-initial stressed:

(158) *Nå kommer hun ikke til å stole på deg lenger.*
 now comes she not to INF trust in you more
 Now she's not going to trust you any more.

Sentence-final stressed:

(159) *Hun kommer ikke til å stole på deg lenger nå.*
 she comes not to INF trust in you more now
 She's not going to trust you any more now.

Continuing the semantic reduction still further, *nå* may be used to make recourse to the fact of the speaker and addressee's common awareness at the present moment, rather than to the actual events which gave rise to that awareness. The utterance is presented as contingent upon the common perspective shared by speaker and addressee at the moment of utterance. This usage occurs with stress, either sentence-initial or sentence-final.

Sentence-initial:

(160) *Nå er ikke jeg noe autoritet, men...*
 now am not I any authority, but
 Now I'm no authority on this, but...

A Functional Analysis of *jo* and *nå*

> *Nå   kunne en   kanskje spørre hvor mye   av dette er sant.*
> now could one maybe   ask   how   much of this is true
> Now one could maybe ask how much of this is true.

> *Ta   deg   sammen   nå,   Frank.*
> take yourself together now   Frank
> Get a hold on yourself now, Frank.

Note that it is in this usage that the phonological reduction begins to be manifested. In all of the examples previous to the one above, *nå* could take contrastive stress (sentence stress), as in:

(161) *Du kan gå nå.*
 You can go NOW. (i.e., It is NOW that you can go and not some other time.)

Contrastive stress does not change the basic meaning of *nå* in any of the examples discussed so far; it merely emphasizes that the utterance with *nå* somehow contrasts with some other alternative. With the usage under discussion here, however, contrastive stress on *nå* is not possible. An utterance with contrastive stress, as in (162), shifts the meaning of *nå* back up the semantic reduction continuum as it were, to where *nå* again functions as a reference to the end-point on a continuum leading up to the present moment. It no longer merely signals speaker and addressee's common awareness at the present moment.

(162) *Nå er ikke jeg noe autoritet...*
 NOW I'm no authority...

Finally, the postverbal modal particle represents the most reduced form of *nå*, both semantically and phonologically. First of all, with regard to its semantic reduction, the element of 'present time' recedes, and we are left with a recourse to the common perspective or consciousness of speaker and hearer. Whether or not such common consciousness in fact exists is not significant; the point is that the speaker, for strategic purposes of his own, is implying or assuming such a common perspective. This recourse may have the effect of adding an appellative element to the utterance. The speaker is appealing to the addressee to accept the force of the utterance because of some implied common perspective. Often the function of the particle cannot be translated lexically, but is dependent on prosodic nuances such as intonation and stress for expression of the equivalent in

English. Phonologically as well, the modal particle shows the most reduction. It may no longer take even word stress.

(163) *Du kan nå alltid prøve.*
you can MP always try
Well you can always try, of course.

Vi er nå pliktig til å stemme.
we are MP duty-bound to INF vote
Well we do have a duty to vote.

The various stages in the semantic and phonological reduction of *nå* are probably not discrete, but represent a continuum upon which the various usages might be plotted as follows.

Deictic time-adverbial—locates proposition at present moment in time.

(164) *Vi kommer nå inn til Oslo sentralstasjon.*
We are now arriving at Oslo Central Station.

Deictic time-adverbial—locates proposition posterior to past events.

(165) *Han er gått—Nå kan du komme ut.*
He's gone—Now you can come out.

Temporal contingency—presents proposition as result of past events, making recourse to addressee's present consciousness of those events.

(166) *Nå kommer hun ikke til å stole på deg lenger.*
Now she's never going to trust you any more.

Present perspective—makes recourse to speaker and addressee's common consciousness at present moment.

(167) *Nå er ikke jeg noe autoritet, men...*
Now I'm no authority on the matter, but...

Common perspective (modal particle)—makes recourse to speaker and addressee's common consciousness.

(168) *Vi er nå pliktig til å stemme.*
Well, we do have a duty to vote.

A Functional Analysis of *jo* and *nå*

4.2.2 The basic meaning of MP *nå*

Whereas the modal particle *jo* only occurs in indicative sentence types, *nå* as modal particle occurs in the interrogative and imperative, as well as the indicative. A look at the effect of the particle on the illocutionary force of each of these sentence types provides some comparative ground for isolating the basic effect of the particle.

Nå in the interrogative. The occurrence of *nå* as modal particle in the interrogative is limited to questions with the actual illocutionary force of an exclamation, such as the following.

(169)   *Har   du   nå   sett   på   maken?!*
        have you MP   seen   at   the^likes
        Have you ever seen the likes?!

   Hva gjør nå det?!
   what does MP that
   What difference does that make?! (i.e., 'Who cares?')

Although in the syntactic form of questions, these are not requests for information. In this regard their effect is more similar to that of rhetorical questions. Instead of soliciting information, they solicit an emotional response. A verse taken from a little cheer used by *Brann*, the local soccer team from the city of Bergen, illustrates this effect nicely.

(170)   *De seier som sant*
        At vi taper iblant;
        Ka bryr du oss med?!
        Vi e best for det!

   Ifjor var det VM
   Og Brann kom 'kje med;
   VM—*pøh!*
   Ka e no det?!

   They say (and it's true)
   That we've lost one or two;
   "Who cares?!" we say,
   "We're best anyway!"

Last year was the World Cup,
but Brann wasn't there;
World Cup—phooey!
What do we care?!

The last sentence, *Ka e no det?* with the modal particle, has the literal meaning 'What is *(nå)* that?' The illocutionary force, however, would be best captured by 'What's the big deal about that?!' Such an exclamation with *nå* expresses the emotion of the speaker, and invites and appeals to the addressee to acknowledge the force of the utterance.

That this emotional appeal is a feature of the *nå* particle is evidenced by the fact that no question that actually functions as a solicitation for information may take the particle.

(171) **Har du nå sett katten min noe sted?*
      have you MP seen cat my any place
      Have you seen my cat anywhere?

Thus the interpretation of the sentence in (172) may not be that the speaker desires to know how his future will be affected if he fails the exam, but rather that the speaker is not inclined to take the exam, and wishes to convince the addressee that this will not make any difference.

(172) *Hva gjør nå det om jeg ikke tar eksamen?*
      what does MP it if I not take exam
      What difference will it make if I don't take the exam?

Nå **in the imperative.** The effect of the particle in imperative sentences may be illustrated in the same way by examining situational contexts where the particle may not occur. The following series of utterances might be spoken by a military commander during battle.

(173) *Lad kannonene!*
      Ta sikte!
      Hold ilden!

      Load the cannons!
      Take aim!
      Hold your fire!

Use of the *nå* particle would change the effect of the utterances dramatically:

A Functional Analysis of *jo* and *nå*

(174) Lad nå kannonene!
       Ta nå sikte!
       Hold nå ilden!

The utterances in (174) no longer have the force of commands. The speaker is now appealing to the addressee(s) to comply with the directives, more along the lines of 'Come on, load the cannons, will ya?'

According to Searle (1969), one of the preparatory conditions on the speech act COMMAND is that the speaker enjoys a social position which gives him the authority to expect obedience from the addressee. In the imperative sentence with *nå*, the speaker is acknowledging that he lacks such authority. He is instead appealing to the addressee's sense of decency or some other motivating factor in an attempt to secure their cooperation. In this case one of the preparatory conditions is being hedged, with the resultant effect that the force of the utterance as a command is weakened to an entreaty.

Now consider the following utterance:

(175) Kom   her   og   se   hva   jeg har   kjøpt til deg.
       come here and   see   what I   have bought to   you
       Come here and look at what I've bought you.

Here the imperative has the illocutionary force not of a command, but more of a casual suggestion or invitation. Again the insertion of the particle has a dramatic effect.

(176) Kom   nå her   og   se   hva   jeg har   kjøpt til deg.
       come MP here and see   what I   have bought to   you

The forces of the two very different utterances might best be captured in English by differences in intonation. However, a possible translation of the second would be '(At least you could) come here and see what I've bought you!'

Here the speaker has reason to believe that the addressee is reluctant to comply. He has shown no interest in seeing what was bought for him, and the speaker finds this unacceptable. The utterance takes on a more impatient tone. In this case the force is strengthened from a simple suggestion to an entreaty or an appeal.

So we have examples of *nå* both weakening and strengthening the illocutionary force of the utterance, in both cases by adding an appellative element. The nature of an appeal is that it attempts to secure acceptance of the proposition by the addressee. This it does, not by overwhelmingly convincing him against his will, forcing itself upon him, so to speak, but by resorting to some shared perception or value which might cause the addressee to willingly accept the illocutionary intent of the utterance.

This correlates with the hypothesis made above as a result of the discussion on the semantic reduction of *nå*. The particle signals a recourse to a consciousness or perception common to speaker and addressee. Dependent upon the social context and their relative status, this contingency upon common values or awareness of speaker and hearer may in some cases serve to weaken the imperative force of the utterance, in other cases to strengthen it.

The following textual examples illustrate the appellative effect of the particle in imperative sentences. The participants in each of the exchanges are on familiar terms with each other. They are peers, none holding any position of authority or prestige with respect to their interlocuters.

(177) (JH76-1)
(R, B, and others have just presented the news that H is elected to the city council. He doesn't believe them.)

H: *Ka e dette for en komedie.*
R: *De e ingen komedie, Herwitz. Imorgen får dokker de høytidelige dokumentene, men (anstrengt gemyttlig) vi ville være først i mål te å berede dokker, så dokker ikkje skulle få begavninger, om budskapet kom for plutselig.*
B: *Alvorlig talt: No må du då for fankeren skjønne, ka vi mener med deg. Se no litt glad ut.*

H: What kind of comedy is this?
R: It's no comedy, Herwitz. Tomorrow you'll get the official documents, but (with effort to be jovial) we wanted to be the first to warn you, so you wouldn't have a heart attack if the news should come too suddenly.
B: For crying out loud, you've got to understand what we're trying to say. Look *(nå)* a little cheerful.

(178) (JH8-1)
A: *Jaja, Herwitz far, eg vikkje forstørre deg i din vemodighet—men jaggu e det akkurat som vi skulle vere på graven. Det ikkje annt enn minnekaffi og minnesokker og minnepale...*
B: *(mot ham) Bøschen.*
A: *Nei far no ikkje opp. Det var kje slik ment.*

A Functional Analysis of *jo* and *nå*

A: Okay Herwitz, I won't disturb you in your sadness—but damned if this isn't just like being at a funeral. Nothing but memorials...
B: (turning to him) Bøschen.
A: Now don't *(nå)* get upset. I didn't mean it like that.

The speakers in the above exchange are brothers-in-law. A's final utterance here has the force of an entreaty. He appeals to B to not get upset, offering a conciliatory 'olive branch' in saying that he didn't mean to offend.

(179) (JH10-2)
A: *No står du og flirer, ja. Flire og jeipe, det har du og kollegene dine alltid vært god te.*
B: *Jaja, Herwitz, la oss være glad så lenge vi kan flire. Så tyter vi ikkje den stunden.*
A: *Og så gir du en god dag i om andre tyter—ja om fliret ditt tar livet av de.*
B: *Uff. Kom no ikkje med dette sludderet.*

A: You stand there with that mocking grin. Grin and stick your tongue out—you and your colleagues have always been good at that.
B: Well, Herwitz, let's be glad that we can grin. At least then we're not complaining.
A: And you couldn't care less if other people are complaining, or how many people you kill with that grin of yours.
B: Oh... Don't give me *(nå)* that garbage.

The *uff* in B's final utterance (somewhat inadequately translated 'Oh...') is the type of expletive that might typically be accompanied by a wince, a grimace, and a turning of one's head to the side, as if one has encountered something distasteful. Here B is signalling that he has been affected emotionally in a negative way by A's utterance. That he overtly signals this emotional vulnerability to the addressee indicates the desire for cooperation, for reaching a consensus. The utterance with the particle continues this emotional expression, appealing to the addressee based on recourse to some assumed or implied common perception.

In the next example, the respected doctor comes to the door for a social call. He is later than the agreed-upon time, and apologizes, saying he had to see a patient. The housewife who answered the door excuses him, asking if it was anything serious, to which he replies that he has come from assisting with the birth of twins. More conversation follows while the two remain standing at the door. Suddenly, during her own conversational turn, the housewife realizes that she is being less than polite by not asking the doctor to come in. She then makes an abrupt transition from discussing the birth, and utters the following:

(180) (JH33–1)
Jaja, kom no inn og få nokke å størke
well come MP in and get something to strengthen

Dem på.
yourself on

The utterance has the force of an invitation. The appelative effect of the particle with the imperative gives the invitation more force, strengthening it from an invitation to more of an entreaty, along the lines of 'Well DO come in and have something to eat.'

Having identified the function of the particle in imperative and interrogative sentences, we now turn to the most frequent particle context—the indicative. It is here that the particle shows the greatest diversity of effects. Yet each of these various nuances, it is suggested, has at its roots this basic element of recourse to shared perception or values.

Nå in the indicative. The first and most obvious characteristic of *nå* in the indicative is that it is never used when the speaker is merely conveying information. The following utterance would never be heard on a radio or television newscast for example, whose purpose is solely to impart information.

(181) *President Zia var nå drept i en flyulykke.*
President Zia was MP killed in a plane^crash.

The above utterance implies some sort of commentary. The listener gets the feeling that the speaker has some other point to make besides just the information contained in the proposition. Such a commentary requires some sort of prior linguistic or situational context upon which to base its interpretation.

Consider now the following situation: an accused killer after taking the witness stand confesses to the murder. When asked why he did it he replies, 'Just for fun'. At this point the enraged mother of the victim shouts from her seat in the courtroom:

(182) *Du er gal!*
 You are mad!

She would not, however, say:

(183) **Du er nå gal!*
 You are *(nå)* mad!

After leaving the witness stand, however, and taking his seat in the courtroom, the defendant's lawyer leans over and speaks to him, initiating the following exchange:

(184) L: *Korfor gjorde du det?*
 D: *Hadde bare lyst.*
 L: *Du e no ikkje riktig vel bevart.*

 L: Why did you do it?
 D: Just felt like it.
 L: You're *(nå)* not normal.

Where the mother's utterance could not take the particle, that of the lawyer could. The difference here is not degree of emotion. The mother may have spoken softly or mumbled under her breath, while the lawyer might have shown the greatest disgust. The crucial difference is that in the second example there is *dialogue*. The lawyer is making the illocutionary force of his utterance contingent on the acceptance of the addressee, in effect saying, 'YOU'VE GOT TO ADMIT THAT you're not normal'. In the first example, on the other hand, there is no dialogue between speaker and hearer. The mother is signalling that the force of her utterance is not negotiable, something to the effect of, 'I DON'T CARE WHAT YOU SAY, you're mad!' She is not making the force of the utterance contingent upon its acceptance by the addressee, but rather, as it were forcing it upon him.

Consider a further example. All passengers are aboard an airliner and seated. The boarding gates have been closed. A passenger suddenly remembers that he has forgotten something, and asks one of the stewardesses if he may leave the plane. If the stewardess replies directly with a negative answer, she would use the utterance in (185) without the particle, not the one in (186).

(185) *Nei, flyet tar av om fem minutter.*
 No, the plane will take off in five minutes.

(186) *Nei, flyet tar no av om fem minutter.
No, the plane will (nå) take off in five minutes.

The stewardess is not making the force of her utterance contingent on its acceptance by the speaker. She is making a nonnegotiable, direct rejection of the request.

If the stewardess, however, should choose to reply indirectly, leaving to the speaker to interpret the negative answer contained in the IMPLICATURE of her utterance, she MAY use the *nå* particle.

(187) Vel, flyet tar no av om fem minutter.
Well, the plane will (nå) be taking off in five minutes.

The particle is not obligatory in this second example. The point, however, is that the particle is not compatible with contexts where the speaker is as it were 'forcing' the utterance upon the addressee.

As we saw with the imperative and interrogative, the effect of the *nå* particle is to signal that the speaker is appealing to something which he hopes will cause the addressee to accept the force of the utterance. The discussion on the semantic reduction of *nå* from temporal adverb to modal particle would suggest that the thing which the speaker is making recourse to is some assumed or implied common perception between speaker and addressee.

Note that the stewardess's reply, although literally nothing more than an informational assertion as to the time of takeoff, functions indirectly as a denial of the passenger's request. A correct interpretation of the utterance is not available through linguistic decoding alone, but relies on an understanding of the conversational implicature of the utterance in context. This is possible only through some degree of shared understanding as to the cooperative nature of conversation (cf. Grice 1975). Interestingly, a similar claim is being made here for the *nå* particle, i.e., it signals the speaker's reliance on some shared perspective. However, the force of the above utterance as a denial of the request is not solely an effect of the particle. If the particle were removed, the utterance would still function as an indirect denial. We have not, in the above case, isolated the indirect force of the utterance as an effect, or implicature of the particle. There are, however, other contexts where the presence of the particle CAN be shown to carry certain conversational implicatures.

(188) (RT5)
Pappa og eg er på hytto. Det er så stille og fredelig. Klokka er ni søndag morgon. Skoddo heng nedover fjellsidene. I går letta ho mot kveld.

Dad and I are at the cabin. It's so quiet and peaceful. It's nine o'clock on Sunday morning. The fog is hanging over the mountainside. Yesterday it lifted towards evening.

The final sentence, 'Yesterday it lifted towards evening,' is merely informational as it appears above. *Nå* may be added to this sentence, however, with the result that the sentence immediately takes on an additional implicature as follows:

(189) *I går   letta   ho no mot   kveld.*
yesterday let^up it MP toward evening
Yesterday it lifted toward evening SO I HOPE IT WILL DO THE SAME TODAY.

Note that the same implicature might be conveyed in English without the addition of the capitalized portion above, by means of contrastive stress on 'yesterday' and possibly nonfinal intonation on 'evening'. Consider another example:

(190) (RT28)
Hilde har hatt lungebetennelse og var verkeleg dårleg. Onsdag for ei veke sidan... hadde hun over 40 i feber. Pappa køyrde til byn etter medisinen så ho fekk første dosen om kvelden. Fredag skulle ho til kontroll...

Hilde has had pneumonia and was really sick. Wednesday, a week ago, she had a fever of over 104. Dad drove to town for medicine, so she took her first dose in the evening. Friday she had a doctor's appointment.

Here the *nå* particle may be added to either or both of the last two sentences. In the first sentence, the presence of the particle conveys the following implicature:

(191) *Pappa køyrde til byn etter medisinen, så ho fekk no første dosen om kvelden.*

Dad drove to town for the medicine, so she took *(nå)* her first dose in the evening, SO SHE SHOULD BE GETTING BETTER SOON.

Likewise, in the second sentence, the particle conveys an implicature.

(192) *Fredag skulle ho no til kontroll.*

She was *(nå)* going to see the doctor on Friday, SO SHE IS IN GOOD HANDS.

What we have in the above examples, then, are clear cases of contrast where utterances without the particle do not convey the implicature, while utterances with the particle do. The particular implicature is clearly an effect of the presence of the particle, together with the particular context and literal force of the proposition.

However, just because a particular meaning is due to the presence of the particle, that does not justify our saying it is part of the meaning of the particle. Clearly, this would result in a different meaning for the particle in every single context in which it was used. Rather, viewing the basic meaning, i.e., conventional implicature of the particle as 'recourse to a common perception', as suggested above, we may derive the conversational implicature of the utterance with the particle.

By means of the particle, S signals a recourse to some assumed or implied common perception between S and H. This has the effect of making the force of the utterance contingent upon H's willingness to recognize this common perception and accept the force of the utterance on that basis. Such recourse conveys certain implicatures pertaining to the strategy of the speaker in uttering the proposition, i.e., what he wants to accomplish with it. These strategies are often translatable into implied propositions, indicated by small caps in the above examples. In other cases the strategy may translate into emotional or attitudinal nuances. Li and Thompson show this happening with the Chinese sentence-final particle *le*; the particle may express annoyance or irritation, yet this is a secondary result of the primary function of the particle—indicating a "currently relevant state"—in combination with a particular type of speech situation (Li and Thompson 1981:261). The various functions of the particle are conversational implicatures triggered by the conventional implicature of the particle in combination with the pragmatic context. In the next section we examine some of the conversational implicatures conveyed by the *nå* particle.

4.2.3 Emotional and attitudinal effects

By signalling dependence upon the control of the addressee, the speaker may accomplish two very different and even opposite basic implicative effects. In the first group of implicatures described below, the use of the particle has the effect of weakening or softening the force of the utterance. In the second basic group below, the particle has the effect of strengthening the force of the utterance. Finally, the speaker may use the particle in a way which would weaken the force of the utterance, but by doing this in an ironic way, actually manages to strengthen its impact.

Weakening. In general, the weakening *nå* has the effect of conveying a casual attitude towards the utterance. It may signal that the speaker is merely making an incidental comment, an aside. In this case there may be syntactic clues, such as couching of the proposition in a parenthetical clause or adposed sentence margin, as in the following examples.

(193) (JH7-1)
(The speaker is reminiscing sadly about his deceased mother.)

Mens hon satt her og eg satt der i sofaen—vi hadde no forresten klaffebord med voksduk i den tiden—så en dronning satt hon her og øste opp fiskesuppen. Og alltid har vi pale på hinnes mindedager...

While she sat here and I sat there in the sofa—we had *(nå)*, by the way, a folding table and a wax tablecloth in those days—like a queen she sat here and served the fish soup. And we always have perch in her memory...

(194) (JH70-1)
(M is pressing H to admit that something out of the ordinary is going on. He finally admits...)

H: *Nei, I kan gjerne få vite korlissen det henger i sammens— og dokker også småtøser, skjønt eg hadde no ikkje tenkt å fortelle dokker det før alt var klappet og klart... jau, eg holder på å selge...*

H: Well okay, you might as well know what it's all about—
you too you girls, though I hadn't *(nå)* planned on telling
you until everything was ready... I'm going to sell...

In a 'whether or not...' structure, the particle signals the unimportance of the conditions, reinforcing that the main-clause proposition is indeed true in either case.

(195) (JH6-1)
Nei, koselig e han neggu ikkje. Gudskjelov, at her ikkje e flere mindemiddager vi skal feire hos han. For like vemodig e han, enten det no e gebursdag eller brøllopsdag eller døsdag han ska ha oss me te.

No, he's sure as heck not a jovial fellow. Thank God that there aren't any more memorials to celebrate with him. He's just as downhearted whether it's *(nå)* a birthday, wedding anniversary, or funeral he's invited us to.

In an emotionally negative situation for the speaker, the casual attitude may signal resignation or indifference, as if the information contained in the proposition is not significant enough to be upset about.

(196) (JH43-3)
(The speaker has just overheard his friends mocking him behind his back.)

... *no vet eg altså kor eg har dokker... skjønt det har eg no visst før...*

... now I know what you think of me... although I have *(nå)* known that before...

The particle may be used to convey that the speaker is not taking his utterance or the speech situation very seriously, for example, in order to soften an utterance which the speaker feels might be interpreted as a challenge.

(197) (JH78-1)
(C and B are trying to convince H that at last they have given him his due place on the city council. C puts the blame for the delay on others in the city council, B directs some of the blame back to him.)

C: *De skal se det som det er. Deres medborgere føler det er gjort Dem og Deres far stor urett. Den vil de gjøre god igjen. For lenge siden skulle dette vært gjort—men jamen er det stor skam at jeg skal grave meg ut på rådstuen og agitere i ganger og avlukker før dere kan få gluggene opp...*
B: *Å, hr. tollinspektør. I har no ikkje hatt gluggene så svært åpne, I heller.*

C: We'll tell it like it is. Your fellow citizens feel that a great injustice has been done to you and your father. They want to make good for that. This should have been done a long time ago—and it's a big shame that I have to go out agitating in the hallways of the city hall before these people can get their eyes open...
B: Oh, Mr. Customs Inspector. You haven't *(nå)* always had your eyes so wide open either.

(198) (KK-2)
Så no har eg vore gift i vel eit halvt år. Dei seier det skal vere vanskeleg, særleg det fyrste året. Men eg synest no det går bra. Vi har vel ikkje sveva på skyer heile tida, men eg kan ikkje sjå at vi har hatt nokon verkeleg store kriser.

So now I've been married for over half a year. They say it's supposed to be difficult, especially the first year. But I think *(nå)* it's going well. I guess we haven't been floating on clouds the whole time, but I can't see that we've had any really big crises.

The particle may be used to respond to a negative remark with a joke.

(199) (JH43-1)
(H turns out to have heard all the negative comments the others were making about him when they thought he was asleep.)

W: *Hr. Herwitz...*
H: *Ja takk—"Hr. Herwitz"... Nei, De behøver ingenting å si ...I har sagt nok.*
B: *(forsøker å ta det gemyttlig) Og du har logge der og lyttet? Det var no egentlig lumpent ut av deg, svoger.*

W: Mr. Herwitz...
H: Right... "Mr. Herwitz"... No, you don't have to say a thing... You have said enough.
B: (trying to take it with good humor) And you've been lying there listening? That was *(nå)* really quite nasty of you, brother-in-law.

(200) (JH5-2)
A: *Å, du kje lett å vere sammens med, Herwitz.*
B: *Eg vet det, og klarer du det ikkje, så får du bare sei te, å eg får 6 ensomme dager te om året. Eg har 360 på forhånd.*
A: *Det e no bare i skuddårene. Ellers har du bare 359... hahahaha.*

A: Well, you're not so easy to be with, Herwitz.
B: I know that, and if you can't take it, just let me know, and I'll have 6 more lonesome days a year. I have 360 already.
A: That's *(nå)* only in leap year. Otherwise you only have 359... hahahaha.

The casual attitude conveyed may signal that the utterance represents something to be expected.

(201) (RT103)
Igår slo pappa graset på Neset. Dei i Nesjane har no slått mesteparten ellers.

Yesterday Dad cut the grass out on the point. Otherwise the folks from Nesjane have *(nå)* cut most of the rest.

(202) (RT98)
(mother talking about her son)

Dei var så imponert over Jostein. "Tenk han kom og besøkte oss og satt og prata med oss gamle ein heil kveld," sa Malene, mori. Ja, eg var einig med henne at han var ein fin gutt. Eg måtte no prøva vera litt beskjeden då.

They were so impressed by Jostein. "Imagine, he came and visited us and sat and talked with us old people for a whole evening," says Malene, the mother. Yeah, I guess I had to agree with her that he is a fine boy. I had *(nå)* to be a little bit modest though.

The effect may be to convey that the proposition represents a state of affairs which is 'as usual'.

(203) (RT140)
Eg har vore så doven i dag. Sykla ein tur i Blomsterdalen, men ellers har eg no berre gått her og rota.

I've been so lazy today. Biked in to Blomsterdalen, but otherwise I've *(nå)* just piddled around here.

(204) (RT59)
Farmor er med det same. Ho får no kvalme og oppkast ca. ein gong i veka.

Grandma is the same. She gets *(nå)* queasy and throws up about once a week.

Casualness or nonseriousness may be used to be reassuring. In the following example taken from a personal letter, the writer has just been relating how her granddaughter has been sick. When she then writes that the girl's father is starting his vacation, the use of *nå* indicates that she is not overly concerned about the situation and that things are bound to improve. Thus the particle in this context triggers an implication that the father, and possibly the whole family, has been under too much stress, and that this may somehow be partly responsible for the girl's illness, and further, that his starting vacation is likely to help the girl get well.

(205) (RT45)
Jan Kåre fekk no ferie frå i går, så då kan dei vel slappa meir av.

Jan Kåre started *(nå)* his vacation yesterday, so now I suppose they can relax a bit more.

The particle is also used in speech-acts of admitting or conceding, with the effect of conveying that the speaker does not regard the concession or admission as terribly serious. In English a similar hedged-concession effect might be achieved by saying, 'I guess' such as in 'Oh, I guess I got a little carried away there...'

(206) (JH62-1)
(L, B, and the group are apologizing to H.)

H: *Det var jammen pent av dokker at dokker ville gjorre det forste skrittet.*
B: *Ja, sånn e vi.*
H: *Eg tok litt for tungt på det med det samme. Dokker vet korlissen eg er.*
L: *Vi var no litt uvorne . . . i mu'n. (de andre stemmer i)*

H: It sure was nice of you to take the first step.
B: Well, that's just how we are.
H: I took it a little too seriously at first. You know how I am.
L: We were *(nå)* a little loose-lipped. (the others agree)

(207) (RT26)
Eg synest ikkje ho har same farten som før, men så er ho no snart 81 år.

It doesn't seem to me that she's getting around as well as she used to, but then she *is (nå)* almost 81 years old.

Appellative-emphatic. In the above examples, by signalling recourse to some common perception between speaker and hearer the force of the utterance is made contingent upon it being accepted by the addressee. This contingency has the effect of weakening the force of the utterance. In the examples that follow, the same expression of recourse constitutes an appeal to the addressee to recognize the force of the utterance. The result is that the utterance is given added emphasis. While the weakening *nå* conveys something to the effect of, 'Only accept the force of this assertion if you agree by virtue of our common perception', with the appellative-emphatic *nå* the speaker is signalling something to the effect of, 'Considering the perception/awareness which we have in common, SURELY you will accept the force of proposition *p*'. The casual connotation is still just as much present in this type. Its effect, however, is to suggest that the proposition is so obvious and so easily assented to that the addressee, if he is a reasonable person, is certain to accept it. By conveying this idea, the speaker makes it more difficult for the addressee to not accept the proposition—he puts pressure on the addressee in order to manipulate him to accept the utterance.

A Functional Analysis of *jo* and *nå* 107

Manipulation, then, with regards to both *jo* and *nå*, consists of simultaneously making the force of an utterance easier to accept, and making it harder to reject. In the case of *nå*, the former seems to weaken, the latter to strengthen the force of the utterance. Both have as their ultimate goal to manipulate the addressee into accepting the illocutionary intent, i.e., interactional strategy, of the speaker. The development of items like English *just, simply,* and *quite* is analogous; they may function as a softening hedge, as in (208), but may also be used with an emphatic effect as in (209).

(208) Daddy's just a little tired, that's all.
You simply send in the coupon and the vacation's yours.

(209) That's just awful!
That simply won't do.

The phenomena seem to be parallel. By indicating that there is no need for emphasis, indeed even understating, the speaker suggests that the proposition is obviously true and manipulates the addressee to grant it unchallenged. The following are examples of the appelative/emphatic use of *nå*.

(210) (JH5-1)
A: *Nei, Herwitz, far, både Bøschen og jeg har tenkt å bli her, så lenge du vil ha oss...*
B: *Takk ska du ha, Trinemor. Ja eg vet, det e it offer dokker gjerne gjorr. Men det e no bare tre ganger om året eg forlanger det a dokker. Og e det for møkke, så sei te.*

A: No, Herwitz, both Bøschen and I plan to stay here, as long as you want us.
B: Thank you Trine. Oh, I know it's a sacrifice you're making. But it is *(nå)* only three times a year that I demand it of you. And if that's too much, just say so.

(211) (JH36-1)
D: *Ja, det e synd for dokker, dokter, at dokker ikkje e født her i byen.*
H: *Ja, for Bergen—det e no det egentlige og nokke for seg sjøl. Resten e strileland.*

D: Yeah, it's too bad for you Doctor, that you weren't born here in town.
H: Yeah, because Bergen—it really is *(nå)* one of a kind. The rest of the country is boondocks.

(212) (BIV-6)
Det blir så mye slomsete mannfolkprat rundt det å skulle ha unge, så karete på et vis. Jeg innrømmer at jeg reagerer på det, det virker så lettvint. Og svangerskapskurs forteller jeg nå ingen at jeg går på.

There gets to be so much tasteless talk among the guys about having a baby, sort of macho in a way. I admit that I react to it, it seems so casual. And I sure don't tell *(nå)* anyone that I'm going to childbirth classes.

(213) (JH52-2)
M: *Ja, dokker to e altså blitt enige?*
W: *(med et blikk på Annike, som slår øynene ned og flytter seg bort.) Ja, det er vi.*
M: *Men eg synes Annike sa, at De ikkje hadde fridd på orntlig endå?*
W: *Joda ... Annike ville vel ikke fortelle Dem det—men jeg generer meg ikke.*
M: *Nei, det gjør no mannfolk aldri.*

M: Well, so you two have agreed?
W: (with a glance at Annike, who looks at the floor and moves away.) Yes, we have.
M: But I thought Annike said that you hadn't really proposed yet?
W: Oh sure ... Annike probably wouldn't want to tell you—but I'm not shy.
M: No, men never are *(nå)*, (i.e., THAT'S FOR SURE.)

As suggested above, the attitudinal effect of the particle may trigger certain implicatures dependent on the speech situation. The following utterance, produced in isolation without the particle, merely conveys the proposition with no added implicates.

A Functional Analysis of *jo* and *nå*   109

(214) *Vonar de hadde det fint i Seattle.*
     hope you had it good in Seattle
     Hope you had a good time in Seattle.

When the particle is added, however, the effect is to add emphasis, something along the lines of, 'Given our common perception (i.e., some awareness) it certainly holds true that I hope you had a good time in Seattle'.

(215) *Vonar no de hadde det fint i Seattle.*
     hope MP you had it good in Seattle
     Sure hope you had a good time in Seattle.

The recourse to a common perception assumes or suggests that there indeed is a common perception to which recourse may be made. In the above context, this assumption immediately triggers an implicature that there is some bit of information common to S and H which makes the proposition obtain, such as a reason why H should NOT have had a good time in Seattle.

As discussed above, the use of *nå* in the imperative appears to fall under the appellative-emphatic type.

(216) (JH10-2)
    A: *Og så gir du en god dag i om andre tyter—ja om fliret ditt tar livet av de.*
    B: *Uff. Kom no ikkje med dette sludderet.*

    A: But you don't care if others are complaining—or even if your silly grin kills them all.
    B: Aw, come on. Don't give me *(nå)* that garbage.

However, indicative sentences may convey this appellative element if they have the illocutionary force of entreaties or requests.

(217) (JH78-2)
    (standing at the doorway)
    C: *Har De ikke fått* Dansk videnskabelig Tilskuer?
    H: *Nei.*
    C: *Nå, så må jeg altså fortelle Dem det også.*
    H: *Ka e det—?*

C: *De kunne nu gjerne by meg en stol, når De vet for noen ben jeg står på.*
H: *Å undskyld...*

C: Haven't you gotten the *Danish Scientific Observer?*
H: No.
C: Well. So I have to tell you about that too.
H: What is it—?
C: You COULD *(nå)* offer me a chair, considering what kind of legs I'm standing on.
H: Oh pardon me...

(218) (JH40-1)
D: *Idag skulle De sitt han, dokter. Idag stod han i flor.*
B: *Å doktoren har sitt han i flor forr han. Ka, dokter? Å gubbevare meg vel.*
W: *Nå, nå, hr. Bøschen. Hahaha... husk på...*
D: *Så De har alt vært ani han, dokter? Ja, ikkje han snodig? Te vise frem for en ort og tolv? Ka?...*
W: *Nei, Bøschen. Herwitz var så forekommende og elskverdig mot meg at... men...*
H: *Oss behøver dokker ikkje å genere dokker for, vi kan både han og faren.*
B: *Men De kan no i det minste sie, ka De mener om den boken De fikk?*

D: Today you should have seen him, Doctor. Today he was in rare form.
B: Oh the doctor has seen him in rare form before. Huh Doctor? Oh bless me.
W: Now now, Mr. Bøschen. Hahaha... remember...
D: So you have already met him, Doctor? Isn't he a strange one? Fit for a sideshow, huh?...
W: No, Bøschen. Herwitz was so proper and amiable toward me that... but...
H: You don't have to worry about us, Doctor, we know both him and his father.
B: But at least you can *(nå)* tell us what you think about the book he gave you.

A Functional Analysis of *jo* and *nå*

Ironic. As was discussed above under WEAKENING, the speaker, by using the *nå* particle to purposefully understate the illocutionary force of an utterance, may give the impression that he does not have much at stake in whether the force of the utterance is recognized or not. This may be used in a distinct type of speech situation in which it is clear that the speaker is in fact wishing to emphasize the proposition. Here the speaker is accomplishing his goals by means of irony:

(219) (JH48-1)
(M has just given A a letter from the man she loves but whom her father has forbidden her to see.)

> M: *Men det sier eg deg, Annike, at det e forste og siste gang eg gjør meg te brevdue. Det tar en ende med forskrekkelse for oss alle tre.*
> A: *Han kommer på Harmonistenes konsert torsdag, han også. Han vil nøyes med et blikk og et umerkelig nikk.*
> M: *Han? Nøyes med it blikk og et umerkelig nikk. Jamen sa eg smorr. Nei, eg har no sitt en viss mannsperson svermendes gjennom gaten og kike opp te vindøgene mang en god gang.*

> M: But let me tell you this, Annike. This is the first and last time I'm going to be your messenger. It'll have a terrible end for all three of us.
> A: He's coming to the symphony Thursday too. He will be satisfied with a glance and a discrete nod.
> M: Him? Satisfied with a glance and a discrete nod? Good grief! No, I just happen *(nå)* to have seen a certain man wandering down the street and glancing up at the windows many a time.

(220) (GF-1)
Sitter nå her med morraskaffen min og hjertet i USA. Nils-Gunnar befinner seg i Atlanta og jeg har blitt fullstendig overmannet av ensomhet og anger, å ikke være med på si egen bryllupsreise er lite festlig.

Well, here I sit *(nå)* with my morning coffee and my heart in the USA. Nils-Gunnar is in Atlanta and I have been totally overcome by loneliness and regret—to not be along on your own honeymoon isn't very fun.

4.2.4 Summary

The basic function of *nå* is to make recourse to an implied common perspective between speaker and addressee. This conventional implicature (cf. §4.1.8) is in turn translated within specific interactional contexts into conversational implicatures. The latter may, depending on the context, take the form of emotional and attitudinal effects, or they may be interpreted as implicatures with actual propositional content.

5
Discussion and Conclusions

5.1 Modal particles versus sentence adverbials

The original problem presented in chapter one was that of distinguishing the modal particles from modal adverbs. Several criteria were given which separate the two classes. However, the more significant question was postponed, which may be stated as follows: Do the speaker's comment adverbs and the modal particles have as similar a function as it appears, and if so, why do they exhibit such dramatically different characteristics with regard to stress and syntactic distribution? In the previous chapter we saw some of the complexity of the functions of the modal particles, suggesting that this was quite different from the relatively overt and straightforward function of modal adverbs. In chapter two we suggested that the modality involved in modal particles, being a superordinate modality, or an "assessment of an assessment" (Weydt 1969:64), is of a qualitatively different kind than that of modal adverbs.

Palmer (1986:16), following Lyons, defines modality as "the grammaticalization of a speaker's (subjective) attitudes and opinions." Although the modal particles clearly fall under such a definition of modality, from the preceding discussion it is clear that the modal particles also differ in several ways from other expressions of modality, specifically the modal adverbs. Though their function seems to fall under Givón's speaker's comment adverbs in that they express the speaker's attitude toward or subjective comment on the proposition, the way in which the modal particles accomplish this seems to be much more subtle than the modal adverbs. Modal particles exhibit a function much closer to that of gestures and prosodic features such as stress, intonation, and rate of speech, than to other more classic expressions of modality (cf. Schubiger 1972).

Krivonosov (1977:187) characterized the former as subjective modality, which he equated with "connotative meaning," as opposed to "objective modality" (cf. §2.1.2).

R. Lakoff (1972:910, 920) distinguishes between "implicit" and "explicit" or "covert/tacit" versus "overt" information in discussing the different communicative effects of Japanese expressions as opposed to their English translation. The same distinction would appear to capture the modality difference: modal particles are an implicit or covert expression of the speaker's attitude, while modal adverbs are explicit and overt. In this section the claim will be made that the differences in syntactic distribution are at least in part a result of these functional differences.

5.1.1 Iconicity

According to Givón, the goal of a functional-typological approach is to come to a "systematic understanding of the relation between structure and function" (1984:31). This is made possible by the fact that the form-function relationship is not totally arbitrary, that it is governed by certain "iconicity principles" or "principles which govern natural form-function correlations" (Givón 1984:30).

The iconic form-function relationship applies to morphology, in that grammatical or inflectional morphemes tend to cluster around or cliticize to stems with which they are most closely associated. Thus, for example, number categories tend to be realized as an affix to nominal stems, while mood and tense are realized as verbal affixes.

Givón further applies the idea of iconicity to the syntagmatic arrangment of unbound lexical items. In chapter one the claim was presented that the syntactic position and word-order flexibility of adverbials could be predicted on the basis of semantic scope. Items with a wider scope would be expected to show the greatest positional freedom.

The Norwegian speaker's comment adverbs show a relatively free distribution, in agreement with the prediction. The modal particles, however, although they also have the entire speech situation within their scope, defy the prediction, being restricted to postverbal position within the clause.

It is the purpose of the remainder of §5.1 to show that functional and historical differences between the modal particles and speaker's comment adverbs account for their differences in syntactic distribution.

5.1.2 The three functional realms

Givón distinguishes three major "functional realms" which are coded in language: (a) lexical semantics, (b) propositional semantics, and (c) discourse pragmatics.

Lexical semantics is the realm of concepts, stored in the lexicon and encoded in sequences of sounds. This level Givón refers to as "meaning."

Propositional semantics involves concepts joined together in propositions, syntactically encoded as sentences. This is the realm of "information."

Finally, discourse pragmatics involves the "sequencing or placing of atomic propositions within a wider communicative context, i.e., in discourse." Encoded in this realm are three major components.

SPEAKER'S GOALS: The speech-act values (information, question, command, etc.) as well as other communicative and pragmatic goals of the speaker;

INTERACTION: The social relation between speaker and hearer, what they owe each other, what they know of each other's knowledge, goals and predispositions;

DISCOURSE CONTEXT: What information was processed in the preceding discourse, what can be taken for granted, what is likely to be challenged, what is important vs. ancillary information, what is the foreground of new information as against what is background. (Givón 1984:32)

Each of the three functional realms is contained within the realm on the next level. Words contain meaning, but convey no information unless plugged into a proposition. Likewise propositions have discourse function only when they occur within a specific discourse context.

It appears that the modal particles as well as speaker's comment adverbs, when uttered in context, may affect the discourse pragmatic function of the utterance. Value judgments and epistemic hedges, for example, are ways of modifying a proposition to fit the particular discourse context. What the following section attempts to show, however, is that the modal particles, in contrast to adverbs, have ONLY a discourse pragmatic function. Having originated as fully specified lexical items, they have undergone a process of semantic reduction, until they no longer contain any lexical-semantic meaning, nor do they affect the information at the propositional level. It was shown in the previous chapter that the function of the particles is best stated in terms of implicatures. The claim here is that they are PURE implicature. In Krivonosov's terms, they have no denotation, but are pure connotation.

5.1.3 Semantic reduction

Each of the modal particles appears to have been derived from another lexical item with specific lexical meaning and broader syntactic distribution. The stressed near-homophones survive as modern exponents of this original form.

Recall the discussion in §4.2.1 on the semantic reduction of *nå*. To summarize the conclusion, the various stages in the semantic reduction of *nå* fall on a continuum from *nå* as temporal adverb to *nå* as modal particle. The various usages might be plotted as follows:

Deictic time-adverbial—locates proposition at present moment in time.

(221) *Vi er nå kommet til Oslo sentralstasjon.*
We have now arrived at Oslo Central Station.

Deictic time-adverbial—locates proposition posterior to past events.

(222) *Han er gått—Nå kan du komme ut.*
He's gone—Now you can come out.

Temporal contingency—presents proposition as result of past events, making recourse to addressee's present consciousness of those events.

(223) *Nå kommer hun ikke til å stole på deg lenger.*
Now she's never going to trust you any more.

Present perspective—makes recourse to speaker and addressee's common consciousness at present moment.

(224) *Nå er ikke jeg noe autoritet, men...*
Now I'm no authority on the matter, but...

Common perspective (modal particle)—makes recourse to speaker and addressee's common consciousness.

(225) *Vi er nå pliktig til å stemme.*
Well, we do have a duty to vote.

The point is that in the process of semantic reduction from its original meaning, the semantic content of *nå* became increasingly less specific, to the point where there was no longer any lexical meaning (in Givón's sense)

Discussion and Conclusions

left at all. At the same time, and due to the semantic reduction, the scope of *nå* became increasingly wide, until it included not only the proposition but the entire speech situation. The result is that the modal particle now has the same scope as the speaker's comment adverb, while differing from the adverb in that it is devoid of any lexical meaning, functioning purely in the discourse pragmatic realm.

Since the modal particles have no lexical-semantic meaning, it follows that they will have no impact on the propositional-semantic information of the sentence. Bublitz (1978) has shown this already for the German modal particles, when he finds that they have no effect on the truth-condition of sentences. Indeed, this seems to be the consensus of the German literature as reviewed in chapter two. Arndt found that the particles had no SEMANTIC CHARGE. Krivonosov seemed to be referring to the same thing when he claimed that the particles had no LEXICAL MEANING PROPER. Lütten too agreed that the logical form of the proposition was not affected by the presence of the particle.

The same is true for the Norwegian modal particles. Thus, for example, while the adverb *sannsynligvis* 'probably' and the modal particle *nok* have similar functions, only the former may be expressed in terms of modal logic by means of an epistemic qualifier which modifies the meaning of the sentence. The addition of the modal particle leaves the truth value of the sentence unchanged, affecting only the discourse pragmatic function. Here the inadequacy of the term MODAL PARTICLE becomes apparent. We are clearly referring to a different type of modality than that expressed by means of modal adverbs.

We have seen then that the modal particles have been semantically reduced to the point where they carry only a discourse pragmatic function. In the process, and as a result, their scope has been widened until it includes the entire speech situation. Yet we still are left with the problem of their restricted distribution. Originally characterized by a relatively free syntactic distribution, why, as their scope has widened, have they become more closely bound to the verb? The answer, it is suggested below, lies in the fact that semantic reduction is usually accompanied by phonological reduction.

5.1.4 Relevance, generality, and phonological reduction

Like Givón, Bybee views the form-function relationship in human language as partly iconic, even claiming a "strong correspondence between the content of a linguistic unit and the mode of expression it takes" (Bybee 1985:7).

In her view, linguistic expression is determined by two factors: RELEVANCE and GENERALITY. She defines relevance in relation to morphology as "the extent to which the meaning of the affix directly affects the meaning of the stem" (Bybee 1985:4). Relevance of a category to a stem governs the likelihood of its being realized as an affix on that stem.

As in Givón's thinking, this also applies to the syntagmatic arrangement of lexical items:

> The relevance principle ... also applies to elements before they are bound, and while they are still movable in the clause: elements that belong together conceptually will occur together in the clause. (Bybee 1985:211)

Her second factor, generality, correlates with the fact that a major source of inflectional markers is full lexical items. In order for such an item to first cliticize and then become an inflectional affix, it must be sufficiently general so as to "be applicable to a large number of stems of the appropriate semantic and syntactic category." In order for an item to be so general, it must be reduced to the point where it has minimal semantic content. So far this is what we have seen happen with the modal particles. But Bybee shows further that semantic reduction is parallelled by phonological reduction:

> In the passage of a word to a clitic and eventually to an inflection, both its phonological shape and its semantic content must be reduced. (Bybee 1985:17)

What this suggests in regard to the Norwegian data is that the semantic reduction undergone by the modal particles was accompanied by a corresponding phonological reduction, as evidenced by the fact that the modal particles may not take stress. In general, phonological reduction tends to result in the fusion of the reduced item to the lexical item with which it has been configured according to the relevance principle. However, in the case of the modal particles, which are not specifically relevant to any single clausal constituent, being relevant to the entire utterance, it was the phonological reduction process that determined that they would cliticize to some single constituent in the clause.

According to the evidence presented above for *nå*, the lexical sources of the modal particles may have occurred in as many as three places in the sentence: sentence initial, sentence final, and postverbal. The verb, being the clausal constituent most preferred as the bearer of speaker's comment and other modal expressions whenever those are realized as bound morphemes, was the most likely candidate to receive the cliticization of the particles.

Discussion and Conclusions

So while the wide scope of Norwegian modal particles predicts that they would occur in a syntactic distribution as free as that of the modal adverbs with similar function, the semantic reduction they have undergone in order to take on such a wide scope has been accompanied by a corresponding phonological reduction, causing the particles to become partially cliticized to the verb, and therefore restricted in their syntactic distribution.

5.2 *Jo* and *nå*: A comparative analysis

To sum up the analysis so far, both modal particles *jo* and *nå* attempt to achieve consensus by making RECOURSE to some commonality ("common basis of communication," cf. Lütten 1977) between speaker and hearer. *Jo* makes recourse to an epistemic basis, assuming or implying some common knowledge or belief in opposition to an idea in the speech situation. *Nå* makes recourse to a perceptual basis, assuming or implying some common set of values or expectations. Notice that the basic function of *jo* is twofold, involving recourse plus opposition, while that of *nå* involves only recourse. This correlates with the quite different origins of the two particles as discussed above. Whereas *nå* originated as an adverbial modifier to the clause, *jo* has its origins as a separate utterance, external to the clause with which it became fused. *Jo* has thus received its reduced meaning from two sources, the oppositional element from *jo* as polarity-reversing response particle, and the element of recourse to a common epistemic base from the type of given information typically encoded in the clause with which it was construed.

In some contexts, the two particles appear to convey very similar nuances. Consider the following utterance:

(226) (RT6–17)
I går slo pappa graset på Neset. Dei i Nesjane har (MP) *slått mesteparten ellers.*

Yesterday Dad cut the grass out on the point. The folks from Nesjane have (MP) cut most of it otherwise.

Either particle may be naturally inserted in the (MP) slot. With *nå*, the recourse to common perception conveys something along the lines of an 'as usual' or 'as expected' attitude. It might be translated as:

Yesterday Dad cut the grass out on the point. 'Course the folks from Nesjane have cut most of it otherwise.

With *jo,* the recourse is to a common knowledge base. The assumption is that the addressee already knows what is being said. This might be translated as:

> Yesterday Dad cut the grass out on the point. As you know, the folks from Nesjane have cut most of it otherwise.

In this case, then, recourse to common perception and recourse to common knowledge convey very similar implicatures regarding the utterance's intended effect.

In other instances, however, the two particles may have very different effects, as we see from the following example.

(227) (RT6–93)
Han skal ikkje ha ferie no. Det var så mykje som skulle gjerast på Stord og han var glad til. Vonar (MP) *på ferie ein gong etter jul.*

> He's not taking any vacation now. There was so much to be done in Stord and he was just as glad. He hopes (MP) to get a vacation sometime after Christmas.

First of all, the central point of the segment of text here is the assertion 'He's not taking any vacation now'. The following two sentences expand upon this. The first, 'There was so much to be done in Stord and he was just as glad', is an explanation for the assertion. The function of the second sentence, however, is understood differently depending on the choice of particle.

If *jo* is used, the utterance with the particle is understood as supporting the explanation sentence. It might be translated something like:

> He's not taking any vacation now. There was so much to do in Stord and he was just as glad. After all, he hopes to get a vacation sometime after Christmas.

Remember that the supportive *jo* was found to be COUNTERING some idea which the speaker anticipates may exist in the mind of the addressee because of his previous utterance. In this case, the speaker, upon uttering 'He's not taking vacation now', anticipates a hearer reaction something along the lines of 'Oh, that's too bad'. The *jo* proposition, in supporting the explanation, is attempting to counter this anticipated hearer reaction or 'idea in the air'. The speaker is saying,

> It's not really so bad that he's not taking vacation now, because he DOES hope to get a vacation sometime after Christmas.

Discussion and Conclusions 121

Were the *nå*-particle used, the interpretation would be quite different. *Nå* makes recourse to common values or perceptions. The particle-utterance would be understood as signalling that the speaker shares the values or perceptions of the addressee. In this case, because it is precisely those values which caused the hearer's reaction 'Oh, that's too bad', the particle has the secondary result of implying that the speaker also shares this reaction. In other words, the speaker is saying:

> It really IS too bad that he's not taking vacation now, so, understandably, he really hopes to get one after Christmas.

The *nå* particle in this case is the emphatic type. The utterance with *nå* might be translated as follows:

> He's not taking any vacation now. There was so much to be done in Stord and he was just as glad. He sure hopes to get a vacation sometime after Christmas though.

The following diagram summarizes the comparison:

> x = assertion: 'He's not taking vacation now.'
> i = anticipated hearer reaction: 'Oh, that's too bad.'
> p = particle utterance: 'He hopes to get a vacation sometime after Christmas.'

Effects of particle:

> *jo:* based on our common knowledge of *p*, we should abandon *i*.
> *nå:* (primary) based on our common values we can accept or be sure of *p*.
> (secondary) I share *i* with you.

Thus we find that the different basic functions of the particle trigger certain implicatures because of the particular context. Different contexts cause the particle to interact differently with the nuances and implicatures already present in the textual or interactional context.

5.3 Interaction as manipulation

According to Givón, three types of speech acts are most commonly encoded in languages:

(a) Declarative: Transfer of information from speaker to hearer
(b) Interrogative: Request by speaker of information from hearer
(c) Imperative: Attempt by speaker to elicit action from hearer

As Givón would have it, (b) and (c) are "manipulative" in that the speaker is trying to influence or manipulate the behavior of the hearer, while (a) merely involves a "transfer of information." That human discourse is "largely informative" is what makes human discourse unique as opposed to the language of early childhood, or that of the "higher mammals," in which there is no need to transfer information. The "shared background" is already present, so communication can be directed to the real purpose of interaction, i.e., to manipulate.

In adult speech, however, the shared background needs constantly to be updated before manipulation can take place.

> Under such conditions, even granted that the ultimate purpose of the communicative transaction is indeed to manipulate the other toward some target action, the interlocutors must first—and in fact constantly—create, recreate and repair the body of shared knowledge which is the absolute prerequisite for the ultimate communicative transaction. (Givón 1984:248)

So while Givón concedes to the ultimate manipulative purpose of communicative interaction, he holds out the view that declarative sentences are only indirectly related to that manipulative function.

There are two problems with this view. First, if humans function as social beings, attempting to control and influence the behavior of others in order to seek the fulfillment of their own needs and goals, and they do this when questioning, commanding, warning, requesting, advising, and performing all manner of other speech acts, is it likely that suddenly when uttering a declarative sentence, they should function as automatons, merely transferring data from one brain to another? Secondly, even granted that there may be an underlying manipulative strategy for the transfer of information, it is the shared information which forms the basis for manipulation. It is the acceptance of information which will determine whose goals will be met, who will be the controller, whose manipulation will be successful. Why then should such transfer of information be accomplished uncontested and totally on the terms of the would-be manipulator, i.e., the speaker?

5.3.1 The speech act ASSERTION revised

It is interesting to note that in Searle's classification of speech acts, the ASSERTION (equivalent to Givón's DECLARATIVE) stands out as the only speech act to which the interaction between speaker and hearer is not regarded as an essential element or part of the ESSENTIAL CONDITION in Searle's terms.

The essential condition for a REQUEST for example is that it "counts as an attempt to get H to do A." To ADVISE "counts as an undertaking to the effect that A [some future act of H] is in H's best interest." A WARNING "counts as an undertaking to the effect that E [some future event or state] is not in H's best interest" and so on.

The essential condition of an assertion, however, according to Searle, is that it "counts as an undertaking to the effect that [any proposition] *p* represents an actual state of affairs" (Searle 1969:66–67). No mention is made of the interaction between speaker and hearer. Whereas for other speech acts the hearer or addressee is an essential factor, for assertions only the speaker and the proposition are taken into account.

Searle (1969:66–67) posits the following felicity conditions for the speech act ASSERTION:

Propositional content	Any proposition *p*.
Preparatory	1. S has evidence (reasons, etc.) for the truth of *p*.
	2. It is not obvious to both S and H that H knows (does not need to be reminded of, etc.) *p*.
Sincerity	S believes *p*.
Essential	Counts as an undertaking to the effect that *p* represents an actual state of affairs.

Searle comments that unlike the speech act ARGUE, the assertion does not entail attempting to convince. One may simply state something without trying to convince an interlocuter of its truth. But is this true in normal interpersonal interaction? What would be the speaker's purpose in uttering the proposition if he was not interested in the addressee coming to share his belief or knowledge of the particular state of affairs?

Indeed, in Bühler's and later Jakobson's view of language, a given speech act functions on three levels, the REPRESENTATIVE—relationship of utterance to external situation; the EXPRESSIVE—the relationship of utterance to speaker (Jakobson: emotive); and the APPEAL—the relationship of utterance to addressee (Jakobson: conative) (Bühler 1934, Jakobson 1960). However, cf. Halliday 1973, who merges the expressive and appeal aspects into one interpersonal level. As Bühler held, and Bublitz (1978) argues, these three elements are present in every speech act.

Grice viewed human communication (which he called "meaning-nn," or "nonnatural meaning" to distinguish it from "natural" or "iconic" meaning) in terms of the intention of the speaker. Lyons summarizes this view:

> The meaning of an utterance necessarily involves the sender's communicative intention, and understanding an utterance necessarily involves the receiver's recognition of the sender's communicative intention. (Lyons 1977:733)

Searle himself seemed to recognize that the speaker's intention must be viewed in relation to the effect of the utterance on the addressee:

> ... the speaker intends to produce a certain illocutionary effect by means of getting the hearer to recognize his intention to produce that effect... (Searle 1969:60–61)

The question here then is: Is the speaker's intention merely to output informational data, or is it to see the data received by the addressee, and the addressee's belief system or knowledge of the universe updated accordingly? If we accept the latter view as correct, then we must admit that even the assertion is a manipulative speech act. By using it, the speaker intends to modify the belief or knowledge system of the addressee in such a way as to form a consensus, or common basis of belief about the world, albeit on the speaker's terms.

5.3.2 *Jo* and *nå* as hedges on felicity conditions

The modal particles *jo* and *nå* fit into this analysis. The discussion above has shown the implicative effect of the particles to be a recourse to a common basis of understanding. Following Lütten (1977, 1979) we might characterize the particles as CONSENSUS-CONSTITUTIVE, i.e., their function is to make recourse to some real or pretended consensus for the purpose of manipulating the addressee according to the interactional strategy of the speaker. If, however, the speech act ASSERTION makes no essential reference to the addressee, the particles have no place in the analysis. If the essence of an assertion is merely to output information, then the particles in what would be assertions may not be described in terms of the felicity conditions on the speech act. Any time a particle appears in a declarative clause we must find some other type of speech act to characterize it, leaving the designation

Discussion and Conclusions

ASSERTION for only those utterances whose primary function is solely to output information regardless of the intended effect on the addressee.

There is, of course, a type of language in which the purpose of the speaker may be merely the outputting of information without regard to manipulating the behavior or beliefs of the addressee. Something that newscasts, newspaper articles, and other types of formal monologues have in common is that the existence of the addressee is not significant to the discourse. That is, these types of communication function solely on the REPRESENTATIVE plane of language. Information is presented in complete obliviousness to its intended effect on the beliefs or behavior of the addressee. There are, to put it another way, no interactional goals for the utterance. Even such ordinarily hearer-related speech acts such as thanks or warnings are presented in a newscast as pure information: 'Television Station KQRY thanks its viewers...' rather than 'Thank you, viewers' or 'Tornado warnings are in effect', but not 'Watch out for tornadoes this weekend'. (Some newscasters may resort to such informal hearer-including language for the effect of personalizing the broadcast.)

It is not coincidental that the modal particles never appear and indeed would be out of place in such formal, addressee-excluded monologue. Lakoff observed that when particles are used in such formal prose, they tend to be ones like INDEED, which give information about the relationship of elements in the discourse to one another, but not about the relationship of the speaker to the addressee, or the speaker's feelings about the information he is conveying (R. Lakoff 1972:920). Use of an expression involving the speaker-addressee dynamic requires that the speaker have some idea about the relative status of himself and his addressee, the type of social situation in which the exchange takes place, and, as suggested above, possibly also the beliefs, values, or expectations of the addressee. Because such cues are not available in certain types of formal prose unless the speaker chooses to pretend that they are, expressions involving the speaker-hearer dynamic will not be utilized. That the speaker-hearer relationship IS significant to most types of dialogue and even much monologue discourse, is evident from the frequency of such pragmatic devices as the modal particles. Thus a descriptive framework is needed which accounts for the speaker-hearer relationship. Searle's speech-act categories do just this in all but the assertion category.

The conclusion of the argument then is to redefine the assertion along the lines of the other speech acts, in social-interactive terms, rather than defining the assertion in normal discourse purely in terms of transferring information, which would force us to invent some other kind of speech act for assertions with particles. We find that the particles then may be analyzed as modifications or hedges on particular felicity conditions of such a consensus-establishing assertion. The following is a suggested revision of Searle's felicity conditions for an ASSERTION (see §5.3.1), according to a manipulative view of communication.

Propositional content	Any proposition *p*.
Preparatory	1. S believes that consensus is not yet reached between S and H regarding the state of affairs described by *p*.
	2. S believes that the utterance of *p* is likely to contribute to the establishment of consensus between S and H regarding the state of affairs described by *p*.
Sincerity	S desires consensus between S and H regarding the state of affairs described by *p*.
Essential	Counts as an attempt to establish consensus between S and H according to S's belief or knowledge of the state of affairs described by *p*.

According to the view of the assertion as an attempt to establish consensus, the conditions under which this type of speech act may be successfully uttered now no longer relate to the propositional content, but rather to the purpose of the speaker in performing such a speech act within the interactional context.

Note that the old felicity conditions relating to the speaker's relationship to the proposition are effectively subsumed under the new system of felicity conditions. That S believes *p* and has evidence for the truth of *p* is guaranteed by the fact that he desires consensus between himself and H regarding the proposition. The new felicity conditions are wider in scope, however, pertaining not only to the speaker's relationship to the proposition, but also his relationship to the addressee.

Because of this expanded scope of assertions, the consensus-constitutive particles now may be described in terms of hedges or modifications on certain of the felicity conditions.

Jo may be seen as a retraction of the first preparatory condition, that S believes a consensus is not yet reached with regards to the state of affairs described by *p*. *Jo* simply assumes, or takes for granted, such a consensus. Such an assumption has the effect of manipulating the addressee to accept the force of the utterance.

Discussion and Conclusions

Nå may be viewed as a strengthening hedge (cf. Brown and Levinson 1978) on the second preparatory condition. As shown above, *nå* makes recourse to an existing or implied perception common to S and H. It attempts to manipulate the addressee into acceptance of the proposition, by giving the appearance as it were that such acceptance is relatively less costly, i.e., less of an adjustment to H's already existing set of assumptions and beliefs about the world.

Thus, the speaker's strategy in using the *nå* particle is not to pretend epistemic consensus (as with *jo*), but rather to pretend a perceptual or value consensus, the existence of which makes it easier and thus more likely that epistemic consensus will be achieved. By means of the *nå* particle, S is signalling that he thinks it MORE likely (than the absence of a particle would signal) that the utterance of the proposition will result in the establishment of consensus between S and H regarding the state of affairs described or implications thereof.

Both particles manipulate by making ASSUMPTIONS about the addressee. *Jo* assumes that he shares in the speaker's knowledge or beliefs about the state of affairs. *Nå* assumes that he shares in the perspective or values of the speaker. There are two ways in which such assumptions manipulate the addressee.

First of all, the speaker's strategy in communicating the assumption may be to signal 'I give you credit for already knowing *p*'. By paying this compliment to the addressee and thereby attending to his "face-needs" in Goffman's terms (cf. Owen 1983), the speaker makes the utterance and its implications easier for the addressee to accept. The addressee benefits, i.e., gains face from the utterance, and is thereby less likely to challenge it.

The converse, and more negative side to the manipulation, is that by signalling his assumption that the addressee shares in his knowledge or perspectives, the speaker may also make it much harder or more costly for the addressee to contest the utterance or its implications. By 'giving him the benefit of the doubt' so to speak, the speaker implies that the reasonable thing to do is to accept the utterance and its implications. To not do so would be unreasonable. What constitutes the manipulative pressure in this case is that the addressee LOSES face if he CONTESTS the utterance.

While the effect of both particles is to manipulate, the manipulative strategy of each IN RELATION TO THE PROPOSITION is quite different. With *jo* the common epistemic base upon which recourse is being made INCLUDES the proposition which contains the particle. With *nå*, however, the common perceptual base is not describable at all in terms of a set of propositions, but as a set of attitudes, expectations, and values. As a result, the use of *jo* helps guarantee the felicity of the proposition itself, while *nå* secures attitudinal advantages which only advance the felicity of the utterance in the sense that they advance the speaker's total strategy for making the utterance.

5.4 Implications

The preceding discussion has important implications for monologue text analysis. As the analysis of the modal particles has shown, a complete description of the function of certain forms requires reference to the entire speech situation, including speaker and addressee.

Recall the discussion of *jo* in monologue texts. We found that of the various usages of *jo* found in conversation, the supportive, concessive, contra-expectational, and oppositional, only the first two were found in monologue texts. It was even suggested that, normally, the latter two would never occur in monologue because they make reference to extralinguistic factors or speaker-addressee interaction not found in a monologue context. A study of the use of *jo* in monologue texts alone and without the insights into speaker-addressee dynamic made possible by analysis of dialogue, may have led us to conclude that the particle had two functions. The first we might have called the supportive, used to indicate that a clause provides support or grounds for the previous clause. The other might have been the concessive, whose function we might have said was to mark the clause as a retraction of the previous clause. The point is that we would have missed the more significant generalization of the function of the particle if the explanation was solely in terms of units of text, without reference to speaker, addressee, and the extralinguistic context. The more significant function is to counter some idea 'in the air' between speaker and addressee, whether that idea originated as a result of some previous utterance by speaker or addressee, or from the expectations of the speaker in relation to the extralinguistic context.

Likewise Li and Thompson show that the text function of the sentence-final particle *le* is a byproduct of its function in conversation. The basic communicative function of *le* is to signal that a "state of affairs has special current relevance with respect to some particular situation." Li and Thompson give five different types of situations where this function is expressed, all of which are interactional situations between two or more speakers. The primary context for this usage of *le* is to signal the finality of a speaker's contribution to the conversation, i.e., to validate it as "newsworthy" of itself (Li and Thompson 1981:283). However, this same usage often occurs at the end of a story where it signals that the story is now over and the other speaker is free to take the floor. The monologue usage of the particle is a secondary subtype of its interactional function. To describe the particle merely as a story-closing marker or something of that nature would miss the rich nuances of meaning discoverable through investigation of conversational exchanges, and account for only a miniscule portion of the particle's function.

Longacre takes up the problem of affixes and particles which:

> ... continue to defy analysis even at a relatively advanced stage of research. Typically, the native speaker uses such affixes and particles with complete assurance but is unable to verbalize anything very concrete as to their meaning and function. (Longacre 1976:468)

His explanation is that:

> ... almost inevitably 'mystery' particles and affixes of this sort are found to have a function which relates to a unit larger than the sentence, i.e., to the paragraph and the discourse. (Longacre 1976:468)

Yet in the same article, Longacre describes the *'jaacu* particle in Cubeo (Columbia) as marking the "polarity between a question and its response." It also occurs at the beginning of each paragraph as a "reminder that we are continuing to develop a story in response to the question which originally elicited it" (p. 470). What might, via text analysis alone, appear to be describable in terms of units of text such as sentence and paragraph, is seen to have a broader function in terms of the speaker-addressee dynamic. If the speaker seems to be orienting himself to the presence and expectations of the addressee, then an insightful analysis will require the inclusion of the speaker-addressee dynamic as a constraint on linguistic form.

Nor does the interaction between speaker and addressee take place in a void. In Shell's analysis of Cashibo modals the response form *ria* may serve not only to indicate that the utterance is the answer to a question, but to signal a "response to a puzzling situation" (Shell 1975:195). An enlightened analysis requires that we look beyond paragraph and discourse, up to the level of the total communicative situation.

Klammer said that "the primary mode of all discourse is dialogue" (1971:34). Indeed by far the most common purpose to which we apply language is in exchanges wherein two or more persons take turns as speaker and addressee within a given situational context. What is being argued for here is that monologue must not be viewed as something qualitatively different, but rather as an extension of dialogue where one speaker holds the floor for an extended time. The addressee has not left the picture. The speaker still is influenced by his relationship to the addressee and by his assessment of the knowledge, beliefs, or opinions of the addressee. As Klammer expresses it,

> Every utterance, spoken or written, depends for its meaningfulness upon a speaker-addressee relationship ... which is always reflected either implicitly or explicitly within the utterance. (Klammer 1971:36)

Text grammarians typically attempt to explain a given feature of the text by making reference to other features within the text itself. The same theoretical constructs and primitives found helpful in grammatical analysis on the clause and sentence level are extended to cover an entire discourse. Brown and Yule reject this "text-as-product view" as they call it, in favor of a "discourse-as-process" approach, in which they:

> consider words, phrases and sentences which appear in the textual record of a discourse to be evidence of an attempt by a producer (speaker/writer) to communicate his message to a recipient (hearer/reader). (Brown and Yule 1983:24)

Van Dijk concedes that:

> notions like presupposition/assertion and topic/comment must be explained as principles of social information processing in conversational contexts. (van Dijk 1977:206)

Even the topics integral to typical text analysis, such as information structuring, switch reference, and topicalization are conditioned, not by some internalized rules for text generation but by the intentions, attitudes, and goals of the speaker in relation to what he assumes about the intentions, attitudes, and expectations of the addressee.

This view of text as interaction in turn impacts translation theory. The goal of translation is to re-encode the speaker's intention (meaning-nn), termed above an interactional strategy or manipulative intent. This intention is evidenced only partially by means of the propositional content. Stated differently, an ideal translation replicates not primarily the propositional content of the original, but the interactional strategy of the author AS MANIFESTED BY the propositional content BUT ALSO BY OTHER MEANS. Emotional and pragmatic devices such as the modal particles, connotation, and style all take on an importance on a par with propositional content as evidence of the speaker's intention.

References

Arndt, Walter. 1960. "Modal particles" in Russian and German. Word:16.323–36.

Askedal, John Ole. 1987. Sprachtypologische Aspekte norwegischer Partikelstrukturen. ms.

Atkinson, J. Maxwell and John Heritage. 1984. Structures of social action. Cambridge: Cambridge University Press.

Atlas, Jay David and Steven C. Levinson. 1981. It-clefts, informativeness and logical form: Radical pragmatics. In Peter Cole (ed.), Radical pragmatics, 1–61. New York: Academic Press.

Austin, John L. 1962. How to do things with words. Oxford: Clarendon.

Bach, Kent and Robert M. Harnish. 1979. Linguistic communication and speech acts. Cambridge: MIT Press.

Baker, Charlotte. 1975. This is just a first approximation, but... Papers from the eleventh regional meeting of the Chicago Linguistic Society, 37–47. Chicago: University of Chicago.

Bastert, Ulrike. 1985. Modalpartikel und Lexikographie: eine exemplarische Studie zur Darstellbarkeit von DOCH im einsprachigen Wörterbuch. Tübingen: Max Niemeyer.

Baunebjerg, Gitte. 1979. "Das ist *eben* nicht so leicht!" zu den dänischen Entsprechungen von *genau, gerade* und *eben*. In Harald Weydt (ed.), Die Partikeln der deutschen Sprache, 189–201. Berlin: Walter de Gruyter.

——— and Monika Wesemann. 1983. Partikelwörterbuch Deutsch-Dänisch, Dänisch-Deutsch: ein Arbeitsbericht. In Harald Weydt (ed.), Partikeln und Interaktion, 119–129. Tübingen: Max Niemeyer.

Berntzen, Rolf, ed. 1976. Jan Herwitz; gamle bergensbilleder; lystspill i fire akter av Hans Wiers-Jensen. ms.

Brown, Gillian and George Yule. 1983. Discourse analysis. Cambridge: Cambridge University Press.
Brown, Penelope and Stephen Levinson. 1978. Universals in language usage: Politeness phenomena. In E. Goody (ed.), Questions and politeness: Strategies in social interaction, 56–311. Cambridge: Cambridge University Press.
Bühler, Karl. 1934. Sprachtheorie. Jena: Fisher.
Bublitz, Wolfram. 1978. Ausdrucksweisen der Sprechereinstellund im Deutschen und Englischen. Tübingen: Max Niemeyer.
Bybee, Joan L. 1985. Morphology: A study of the relation between meaning and form. Amsterdam: John Benjamins.
Carlson, Lauri. 1984. 'Well' in dialogue games: Discourse analysis in idealized conversation. Pragmatics and beyond 5. Amsterdam: John Benjamins.
Christensen, Lars Saabye. 1986. Columbus ankomst. Oslo: Cappelen.
Cole, Peter and Jerry L. Morgan, eds. 1975. Syntax and semantics 3: Speech acts. New York: Academic Press.
Collinson, W. E. 1938. Some German particles and their English equivalents: A study in the technique of conversation. In German studies presented to Prof. H. G. Fiedler, 106–124. Oxford: Oxford University Press.
Corum, Claudia. 1974. Adverbs... long and tangled roots. Papers from the tenth regional meeting of the Chicago Linguistic Society, 90–102. Chicago: University of Chicago.
———. 1975. Basques, particles and baby talk: A case for pragmatics. Proceedings of the first annual meeting of the Berkeley Linguistics Society, 90–99. Berkeley: Institute for Human Learning, University of California, Berkeley.
Donaldson, Tamsin. 1980. Ngiyambaa: The language of the Wangaaybuwan. Cambridge: Cambridge University Press.
Edmondson, Willis. 1981. Spoken discourse: A model for analysis. London: Longman.
Franck, Dorothea. 1980. Grammatik und Konversation. Monographien Linguistikk und Kommunikationsswissenschaft 46. Königstein-Ts.: Scriptor.
Fraser, Bruce. 1975. Hedged performatives. In Peter Cole and Jerry L. Morgan (eds.), Syntax and semantics 3: Speech acts, 187–210. New York: Academic Press.
Fretheim, Thorstein. 1987. The two faces of the Norwegian inference particle 'da'. ms.

Givón, Talmy. 1984. Syntax: A functional-typological introduction. Amsterdam: John Benjamins.
Grice, H. Paul. 1975. Logic and conversation. In Peter Cole and Jerry L. Morgan (eds.), Syntax and semantics 3: Speech acts, 41–58. New York: Academic Press.
———. 1978. Further notes on logic and conversation. In Peter Cole (ed.), Syntax and semantics 9: Pragmatics, 113–128. New York: Academic Press.
Halliday, M. A. K. 1973. Explorations in the functions of language. London: Edward Arnold.
Harden, Theo. 1983. An analysis of the semantic field of the German particles "uberhaupt" and "eigentlich." Tübingen: Gunter Narr.
Haugen, Einer. 1966. Language conflict and language planning: The case of modern Norwegian. Cambridge: Harvard University Press.
———. 1982. Scandinavian language structures: A comparative historical survey. Minneapolis: University of Minnesota Press.
——— and Kenneth G. Chapman. 1982. Spoken Norwegian. New York: Holt, Rinehart and Winston.
Helbig, Gerhard. 1985. Die Partikeln, zur Theorie u. Praxis der Deutschunterricht für Ausländer. Leipzig: VEB Verlag Enzyklopädie.
Hentschel, Elke. 1986. Funktion und Geschichte deutscher Partikeln 'ja', 'doch', 'halt' und 'eben'. Tübingen: Max Niemeyer.
Heritage, John. 1984. A change-of-state token and aspects of its sequential placement. In J. Maxwell Atkinson and John Heritage (eds.), Structures of social action, 299–345. Cambridge: Cambridge University Press.
Hilgendorf, Brigitte. 1981. Review of Die Partikeln der deutschen Sprache, ed. by Harald Weydt. Linguistics 19:1031–1035.
Jakobson, Roman. 1960. Linguistics and poetics. In Thomas A. Sebeok (ed.), Style in language, 350–77. Cambridge: MIT Press.
James, Deborah. 1972. Some aspects of the syntax and semantics of interjections. Proceedings of the eighth regional meeting of the Chicago Linguistic Society, 162–72. Chicago: University of Chicago.
———. 1973. Another look at, say, some grammatical constraints on, oh, interjections and hesitations. Papers from the ninth regional meeting of the Chicago Linguistic Society, 242–51. Chicago: University of Chicago.
Klammer, Thomas P. 1971. The structure of dialogue paragraphs in written dramatic and narrative discourse. Ann Arbor: University of Michigan.
———. 1973. Foundations for a theory of dialogue structure. Poetics 9:27–64.
Klouman, Sverre. 1984. Learn Norwegian. Oslo: Tanum-Nordli.

Kreckel, Marga. 1981. Communicative acts and shared knowledge in natural discourse. London: Academic Press.
Krivonosov, A. 1977. Deutsche Modalpartikeln im System der unflektierten Wortklassen. In Harald Weydt (ed.), Aspekte der Modalpartikeln: Studien zur deutschen Abtönung, 176–216. Tübingen: Max Niemeyer.
Kuno, Susumu. 1973. The structure of the Japanese language. Cambridge: MIT Press.
Lakoff, Gordon. 1972. Hedges: A study in meaning criteria and the logic of fuzzy concepts. Papers from the eighth regional meeting of the Chicago Linguistic Society, 183–228. Chicago: University of Chicago.
Lakoff, Robin. 1972. Language in context. Language 48(4):907–27.
———. 1973a. Questionable answers and answerable questions. In Braj B. Kachru, et al. (eds.), Issues in linguistics: Papers in honor of Henry and Renée Kahane, 453–67. Urbana: University of Illinois Press.
———. 1973b. The logic of politeness; or, minding your p's and q's. Papers from the ninth regional meeting of the Chicago Linguistic Society, 292–305. Chicago: University of Chicago.
Levinson, Steven C. 1983. Pragmatics. Cambridge: Cambridge University Press.
Li, Charles N. and Sandra A. Thompson. 1981. Mandarin Chinese: A functional reference grammar. Berkeley: University of California Press.
Longacre, Robert E. 1976. Mystery particles and affixes. Proceedings of the twelfth regional meeting of the Chicago Linguistic Society, 468–75. Chicago: University of Chicago.
———. 1983. The grammar of discourse. New York: Plenem Press.
Lütten, Jutta. 1977. Untersuchungen zur Leistung der Partikeln in der gesprochenen deutschen Sprache. Göppingen: Alfred Kümmerle.
———. 1979. Die Rolle der Partikeln 'doch', 'eben' und 'ja' als Konsensus-Konstitutiva in gesprochenen Sprache. In Harald Weydt (ed.), Die Partikeln der deutschen Sprache, 30–38. Berlin: de Gruyter.
Lyons, John. 1977. Semantics. Cambridge: Cambridge University Press.
Matthews, George Hubert. 1965. Hidatsa Syntax. The Hague: Mouton.
Owen, Marion. 1981. Conversational units and the use of 'well'. In Paul Werth (ed.), Conversation and discourse, 99–115. London: Croom Helm.
———. 1983. Apologies and remedial interchanges: A study of language use in social interaction. New York: Mouton.
Palmer, F. R. 1986. Mood and modality. Cambridge: Cambridge University Press.

Prince, Ellen F. 1979. On the given/new distinction. Papers from the fifteenth regional meeting of the Chicago Linguistic Society, 267–278. Chicago: University of Chicago.

———. 1981. Toward a taxonomy of given-new information. In P. Cole (ed.), Radical pragmatics, 223–255. New York: Academic Press.

Rösler, Dietmar. 1982. Teaching German modal particles. Iral 20(1):33–38.

Sacks, Harvey, Emmanuel A. Schegloff, and Gail Jefferson. 1974. A simplest systematics for the organization of turn-taking in conversation. Language 50(4):696–735.

Schecker, Michael. 1980. Was sind—und wozu analysiert man Sprachpartikel? zum internationalen Kolloquium "Partikel und Deutschunterricht." Deutsche Sprache, 2 June, 177–188.

Schegloff, Emmanuel A. 1984. On some questions and ambiguities in conversation. In J. Maxwell Atkinson and John Heritage (eds.), Structures of social action. Cambridge: Cambridge University Press.

Schegloff, Emmanuel A. and Harvey Sacks. 1973. Opening up closings. Semiotica 7(4):289–327.

Schubiger, Maria. 1972. English intonation and German modal particles: A comparative study. In Dwight Bolinger (ed.), Intonation, 175–193. Harmondsworth: Penguin Books.

Searle, John R. 1969. Speech acts. Cambridge: Cambridge University Press.

———. 1975. Indirect Speech Acts. In Peter Cole and Jerry L. Morgan (eds.), Syntax and semantics 3: Speech acts, 59–82. New York: Academic Press.

———. 1976. A classification of illocutionary acts. Language in Society 5:1–23.

———, Ferenc Kieter, and Manfred Bierwisch, eds. 1980. Speech act theory and pragmatics. Dordrecht, Holland: D. Reidel.

Shell, Olive A. 1975. Cashibo modals and the performative analysis. Foundations of Language 13:177–199.

Sperber, Dan and Deirdre Wilson. 1982. Mutual knowledge and relevance in theories of comprehension. In N. V. Smith (ed.), Mutual knowledge, 61–87. London: Academic Press.

———. 1986. Relevance: Communication and cognition. (Language and thought.) Cambridge: Harvard University Press.

Stigen, Terje. 1987. Den røde sommerfugl og 5 andre hørespill. Oslo: Gyldendal.

Stokker, Kathleen and Odd Haddal. 1981. Norsk, nordmenn og Norge. Madison: University of Wisconsin Press.

Trudgil, Peter. 1974. Sociolinguistics: An introduction. Harmondsworth: Penguin.

van Dijk, Teun Adrianus. 1977. Text and context: Explorations in the semantics and pragmatics of discourse. London: Longman.
Van Valin, Robert D. 1975. German 'doch'. The basic phenomena. Papers from the eleventh regional meeting of the Chicago Linguistic Society, 625–637. Chicago: University of Chicago.
de Vries, January. 1962. Altnordisches etymologisches wörterbuch. Leiden, Netherlands: E.J. Brill.
Wesemann, Monika. 1981. Das ist *doch* kein problem: zu den dänischen Entsprechungen der deutschen Abtönungspartikel *doch*. In Harald Weydt (ed.), Partikeln und Deutschunterricht, 238–248. Heldelberg: Julius Groos.
Weydt, Harald. 1969. Abtönungspartikeln: die deutschen Modalwörter und ihre französischen Entsprechungen. Bad Homberg v.d.H.: Gehlen.
———, ed. 1977. Aspekte der Modalpartikeln: studien zur deutschen Abtönung. Tübingen: Max Niemeyer
———, ed. 1979. Die Partikeln der deutschen Sprache. Berlin: de Gruyter.
———, ed. 1981. Partikeln und Deutscheunterricht: Abtönungspartikeln für Lehrner des Deutschen. Heidelberg: Julius Groos.
———, ed. 1983. Partikeln und Interaktion. Tübingen: Max Niemeyer.
———, et al. 1983. Kleine deutsche Partikellehre: ein Lehr- und Übungsbuch für Deutsch als Fremdsprache. Stuttgart: Ernst Klett.
———. 1987. Partikel-Bibliographie: internationale Sprachenforschung zu Partikeln und Interjektionen. Frankfurt: P. Lang.

www.ingramcontent.com/pod-product-compliance
Lightning Source LLC
Chambersburg PA
CBHW070738230426
43669CB00014B/2493